TAROT: THE OPEN LABYRINTH

How the Tarot can help us answer specific questions,
act as a tool for psychological analysis and tell us how
to overcome problems.

TAROT
THE OPEN LABYRINTH

Rachel Pollack

THE AQUARIAN PRESS
Wellingborough, Northamptonshire

To my father

First published 1986

© RACHEL POLLACK 1986

British Library Cataloguing in Publication Data

Pollack, Rachel
  Tarot: the open labyrinth.
  1. Tarot
  I. Title
  133.3'2424   BF1879.T2

  ISBN 0-85030-465-2

The Aquarian Press is part of the Thorsons Publishing Group

Printed and bound in Great Britain

Contents

Preface   7

Introduction   9

1. A Three Card Reading   27

2. The Celtic Cross   35

    Celtic Cross One   38

    Celtic Cross Two   54

    Celtic Cross Three   66

3. The Work Cycle   101

    Work Cycle One   102

    Work Cycle Two   118

    Work Cycle Three   131

4. Meditation   149

    Meditation One: The Fool   154

    Meditation Two: Eight of Cups   156

Preface

Fool's Day, 1985

This book was begun on Fool's Day, April 1, 1985. The Fool in the Major Arcana signifies a willingness to leap into unknown territory, to take risks, to go where instinct tells you and not caution. A book such as this one has many patrons in the 'greater trumps' (as Charles Williams called the Major Arcana): the Hermit for wisdom, the High Priestess for instinct, her partner the Hierophant (sometimes named the High Priest) for teachings, the Emperor for structure, and above all Justice for the courage — and the ability — to see the truth. None of these, however, can come into being without the Fool. For no reading is possible, and no meditation can open up the soul without that readiness to jump into the mystery. And so this book, like all projects of serious intention, belongs to the Fool.

Introduction

Some things we can learn only in the doing. However much we may study the techniques of Tarot reading, we cannot really know them until we start laying out the cards and interpreting them. The learning advances slowly, from the consulting of books and notes to the memorizing of spreads to the moments when we start seeing the connections and forming our own style of interpretation. In this process the example of someone else can help people find their own way. In a previous work (*Seventy-Eight Degrees of Wisdom, Part Two*), I described in some detail approaches to Tarot divination as well as some thoughts about their value and purpose. The brief examples given in that book helped to illustrate the ways in which the techniques can come to life. This book continues that method with a series of readings done by me over the past few years. They come from a variety of situations, from people in crisis to those who simply want to know what the cards can tell them. In each case I have attempted to show how the individual cards form a unique pattern, with each image both a window into itself and a mirror reflecting all the others.

The descriptions and commentaries are not transcriptions of the readings as they were done at the time. I have not attempted to reconstruct those experiences but rather to begin now, using my notes and my memories of the event as the basis for taking each reading as far as it will go. In one or two cases I have used information gained after the event (a follow-up reading, or later actions taken by the person) to illustrate some point from the reading under discussion. Nevertheless, all the commentaries look back on the readings that spawned them, and they all reflect both the actual things said at the time, and the style and manner in which they were done. I have said I have tried to take each reading as far as it can go. This was the same approach when the readings were done; if the advantages of a written text have allowed me to take them even further I have done so in the spirit of the original experience.

This book attempts to show the mind of one reader at work. Instead of organizing the descriptions into a step-by-step linear explanation I have written about them in much the same way I would talk about them with the subject of the reading. This involves a circular or spiral method, swirling down into the images and up into their meaning and application to the person's life. In some readings we begin with an overview, getting a general impression of the cards' message and then going through each card slowly, watching how it looks forward and backward to the others, how the other images (including sometimes cards that do not appear in the actual reading) add to our understanding of a particular card. In other readings one or two cards will emerge as the foundation, with the others built around them, so that we constantly return to them, carrying our perceptions of the different cards back to them to measure against the central symbol. Slowly, with excitement or difficulty or even some pain, we uncover the true reading, teasing it out from the cards and from the hiding places between them.

A Tarot reading lies before us like a labyrinth. At first it may seem impenetrable, a jumble of official meanings from a book, unconnected to each other or to the person they supposedly describe. Sometimes we circle around the outer edges, trying out this or that, until we find the way inside. For the way does lie open. The more we work with the cards, the more we live with them, and learn how they breathe and speak to each other, then the more we can trust that they will lay out a passage for us. It may come in the first picture, say, the Emperor dominating all the other cards, or in an unexpected outcome, or a disturbing relationship between the outcome and the possible outcome, such as the reading in this book where the knight of Cups leads to the queen of Cups reversed. These things form our entry points, and from there we pick our way through the cards, constantly circling back, looking ahead.

Every reader develops her or his own method. When we begin we may copy someone else's, but eventually, as we come to a personal relationship with the cards, so we also form a personal style. These readings show the way one person approaches divination. I do not expect other people to copy this approach, but only hope they will learn from it, discovering through these examples possibilities and ways of seeing.

Readers might find it valuable to compare their own interpretations with the ones given. If you have your own deck lay the reading out in front of you then imagine yourself as being there, imagine working out the meanings and finding a way to explain them to the subject sitting beside you. Consider yourself also as the subject. Imagine yourself in that person's situation and think how you would react to the images and ideas presented in the reading. Doing this will increase your own feeling for the cards, as well as allow you to develop a dialogue between yourself and the given interpretations. And more. By imagining yourself as both reader and subject you discover a vital point about the practice of divination. The reader *is* the subject of the reading. Every reading tells us something new. Besides the information about the person's life we also find new facets in the cards and the way they fit together. We become more skilled in understanding and explaining them, and most important, we learn about ourselves. The power of these images is such that if we open ourselves up to them, if we seek to enter their symbolic world, they will change us. The images seep into us until we begin to look at life and our own predicaments in different ways.

These readings, then, illustrate a certain way of interpretation. They are, first of all, not predictive. No brown-eyed strangers walk out of these cards, no one travels on them to faraway lands. Here and there they may anticipate some development in the subject's life, but by and large they do not try to tell the future. In some cases (I am thinking primarily about the long reading concerning a love triangle) the cards refuse to predict, often just when the person wants to know what will happen. Instead, they insist on returning the person to her or himself. They say in effect, 'Why do you want to know the future? What will you do with it? Do you think it will release you from the present?'

Of course, this is not always the case. I have seen people who steadfastly demanded predictions and usually the cards have supplied them (with greater or lesser refinement). On some occasions, when people have genuinely needed to know what will happen, the cards have helped them. Once a woman wanted to know if her errant husband would leave his girl friend and return to her. This was partly a question of desperate hope and pride, but without this knowledge she could not begin to plan her life. The cards told her very clearly to forget him and begin to live for herself. They answered her question and more, telling her she could do something for herself once she admitted he was gone.

Some time later this woman returned to me with another question. As part of the divorce settlement her husband had bought an apartment for her. Now he had neglected the payments and she faced eviction. The opportunity of another apartment had come her way, but one less attractive , and she didn't want to take it if she thought her ex-husband would pay the mortgage. The cards made it plain she could not count on him. She would do better to move.

Predictive readings then do take place. In general, however, I have not chosen them for this book. Instead, the readings contained here illustrate the Tarot's possibilities for illuminating a person's life. Whether they come from people with a particular problem or those who just want to see what the cards can tell them, these readings share certain characteristics. They all look beyond and within the immediate situation to expose the subject's wider needs and ways of behaviour. Some will demonstrate long standing patterns or cycles in the person's life. Others bring to the surface fears or sorrows that may have limited the psyche for years with little or no conscious awareness. Still others will return the person to the origins of the current situation. And they all point to ways of going forward. If they show problems they also show potentialities. If they describe crises or uncover sorrow they also indicate possible solutions — not easy solutions, and sometimes not even pleasant solutions, but still, ways of continuing.

Not every Tarot reading will bring out such qualities. Another characteristic these examples share is that they come from a 'moment of illumination'. Something unknown (or unknowable) clicks into place and the particular reading stretches beyond the usual descriptions of current influences. We cannot say ahead of time when this will happen. Sometimes the seriousness of the question or the receptive attitude of the subject (and the reader) will seem to bring it about, but there is no guarantee. And at other times — such as the first reading in this book — there was no conscious expectation of deep meaning. In the example just mentioned the woman had laid out three cards in front of her and said, 'What do you think of these?'

The kind of reading shown here requires a certain kind of reader, and also a certain kind of subject. In regard to the reader she or he must know the cards thoroughly, must come to them with respect, and at the same time be willing to wrestle with them, to sometimes pull the interpretations loose instead of assuming they will always lie there on the surface waiting to be plucked. The reader must understand that the Tarot, the reader, and the subject all create the reading between them. He or she needs a high degree of curiousity about the psyche and about psychological principles and the ways in which the psyche reveals itself through behaviour and attitude. And finally, the reader must cultivate a feeling for symbols, the way in which an image can contain a whole network of meanings, and the way in which that network expands each time we enter it. Without this last attitude, the reader will only know various books' descriptions of the cards, and not the cards themselves.

This description represents the ideal reader. Like anyone else, I can only try to develop these qualities. If I have succeeded to any extent then I have had an ally — the Tarot itself. For the cards not only require such skills and attitudes, they also help to create them. The long and serious practice of Tarot readings forms a kind of exercise programme for the mind and spirit.

The subject needs many of the same qualities as the reader. A sensitivity to symbols will allow the reader's descriptions of the images to act as a trigger for the subject's own responses. She or he also needs a measure of self-awareness and honesty, so that when the reader's comments hit home the subject will acknowledge it. She or he must have a concern for self-discovery, a desire to grow, and to confront and overcome problems. Without these qualities the reading may pass by unnoticed, or else become distorted, either into a message of doom or an assurance that everything is fine and nothing needs to be done.

The subjects of these readings tend to share characteristics as much as the readings themselves do. They are people open to ideas, people who will allow images to stimulate their perceptions of themselves and their experiences. They are people who recognize the necessity of change, who accept the challenge of using change, and even pain, as openings to deepen their lives. Many, though not all, have done some study in spiritual discipline. One or two have done some psychotherapy, while a few have worked in the arts. Several have done other readings with me besides the ones described here. In some instances the previous (or following) readings were vital to understanding the one under discussion and so I have quoted them. In others they made little difference and are not mentioned. In one case a reading done by someone else for a third person on the same day proved valuable to understanding 'our' reading and so I have quoted this outside example as well.

Interestingly, more than twice as many women as men appear in this book. When I began to look through my notes for suitable readings I did not look at the distribution of male and female. Only when I'd selected them and noticed the predominance of women did I check through my collection of readings to find that the (im)balance runs throughout. By my sample, many more women desire Tarot readings than men. I suspect that this stems from a cultural rather than a biological bias. Our culture (like virtually all others) assigns certain ways of thinking and behaving to men and others to women.

For men this includes logic, either/or analysis, and a separation of the self from the way one views the world. We call this viewpoint 'rational' or 'realist', though in fact it forms a one-sided approach to life. In women we tend to encourage intuitive and emotional responses to experience. These differences alone would lead more women to seek divination, but there is another factor involved. Our patriarchal society teaches that the male view of the world is correct and the female distorted. Because the 'official' values of society are the same as those assigned to men, many men identify strongly with society's prejudices. These prejudices include the notion that Tarot readings (or astrology, or any form of divination) are 'irrational' and therefore impossible.

For some men, going to a Tarot reader can imply betraying their position as representatives of society. To do so would make them outsiders, and so they defend society's values by denouncing Tarot readings, not just for themselves, but for anyone else. Several times women clients have told me that they could only come during their husband's or lover's working hours, because their men would get angry if they knew about it. Once, in a hotel with a group of people for the weekend, one of the women asked if I would read her cards. We were sitting in the hotel lounge and just as we began the woman's husband came in to see what was happening. As soon as he found out what we were doing he strode across the room to the furthest corner where he made sure to sit with his back to us until he was sure we were finished.

In general, women do not identify themselves with society and its values in the same way as men. Many women already feel themselves outsiders. Feminists may formulate this consciously in their alliance with 'minorities' despite the fact that there are more women in the world then men. Other women may not express the feeling in such explicit terms but still will sense a separation of themselves from society and its values. They will not give up anything by asking for a Tarot reading. They may, if they think about it, consider the concept of divination as outrageous or impossible, but it doesn't bother them, not in a personal way. A woman will laugh and say, 'I don't understand how it works, but I don't really care.'

Obviously these observations will not apply to all men or to all women. Many women will denounce any suggestion of divination as 'superstitious nonsense', while many men abuse astrology by checking their newspaper horoscopes before taking any action. Still, the high proportion of women to men among at least one Tarot reader's clients says something about the relationship of men and women to established values.

Ironically, the Tarot does not champion 'feminine' qualities. It draws heavily on the traditional assignment of certain values to men and others to women, but it uses all these values together to create a symbolic system applicable to everyone. In the Major Arcana certain cards — the Magician, the Chariot, the Emperor — will suggest the 'male principle', while others — the High Priestess, Strength, the Empress — symbolize the 'female'. In the Minor Arcana, Wands and Swords represent masculine qualities, Cups and Pentacles feminine. But any one of these cards or suits may appear in a particular reading for either a man or a woman. The Tarot teaches us the necessity and worth of both approaches to life. Those cards which signify greatest personal development — Justice, the queen of Cups, the Hermit, the World, among others — all feature a blending of male and female symbolism.

As a system of thought the Tarot teaches us to respect both sets of values. Through the practice of readings we discover that one side or the other may predominate at different times in different people, both men and women. Sometimes a reading will indicate a need to redress an imbalance by deliberately encouraging (or releasing) feminine or masculine qualities. If the person has set all attention outwards, to activity and achievement, then the queen of Pentacles or the High Priestess might signify the value of passivity and of appreciating life rather than trying to conquer it. But those who assume the Tarot embodies only the feminine values of intuition and emotion will find it surprising how often these readings recommend a hard analysis of the situation. At a time when many people advise us that we 'think too much' and should trust our feelings only, the Tarot insists on the necessity of discernment, differentiation. But it teaches us as well to balance these methods with intuitive responses based on self-knowledge.

Just as the interpretation of Tarot readings will demonstrate the importance of integrating the male and female 'principles' so the practice of doing readings helps to encourage this integration in the reader. For we need both qualities to understand and explain the cards. The intellect, basing itself on memory and previous study, can discover various possibilities in the image, but only intuition can determine that some of the possibilities apply and not others. Intuition can crack the mould of previous interpretations to find new meanings in the familiar images; but we depend on the intellect to expand and explain those meanings.

Ideally the reading is only the beginning. A reading does two things for the subject. First, it provides information. Second, it awakens the subject's awareness through the images. This is why the reader will often describe the picture ('We see here someone staring sadly at three spilt cups') even though the card lies in front of the person. Knowing the power of the symbols the reader seeks to implant the image in the subject's mind. But once the reading has done what it can, the subject can then begin to work on the actual situation.

This idea of work is essential to the kind of readings in this book. (One of the two layouts used is called the 'Work Cycle'.) For as mentioned above, the reading shows potential developments. It says that under current conditions, with these influences shown here, things will go in this way. But a desirable outcome will not automatically happen, just as we are not prisoners of an undesirable one.

People often ask if a Tarot reading is inevitable, or if free will plays a part. The question is more complex than it might seem. The Tarot teaches us that free will exists at all moments, but often people do not exercise it, even when they think they do. Much of what we do and even think derives from past experiences and the choices we have made before. Our upbringing and education, the defences we create against the world's cruelty and our own limitations, our previous behaviour and the need to justify it, all these possess a great power to direct our actions. Depth psychology, yoga and such esoteric traditions as alchemy or sufism have all shown that unless people deliberately make themselves conscious they will tend to act from subconscious motives (see below, 'Two Notes On Terms' for the distinction between 'subconscious' and 'unconscious'). We think we act freely, from an assessment of needs and restrictions, but in fact much of what we do we are driven to do, sometimes for no real reason other than the continuation of past patterns.

The Tarot helps us become conscious — if we desire it. Through readings, particularly a series of readings, we face some of those hidden controls. One woman in this book saw the way in which past sorrow restricted her attempts to break loose from a cycle of enthusiasm and despair. In another reading the subject saw he could free himself from a series of painful experiences fifteen years earlier. At times readings will show us our self-deception. In the very long reading featuring a romantic triangle, Strength reversed in the position of 'hopes and fears' helped the woman see that she desired weakness because she thought that weakness would compel the other people to do what she wanted without her having to make a decision. The card (plus others, particularly the ten of Wands reversed) helped her recognize her own confused ideas about strength and responsibility. She believed — subconsciously — that being strong required her to accept situations that hurt or distressed her. Only weakness could free her.

The reading helped her overcome this idea by bringing it to her attention. She would have made a mistake, however, if she assumed that knowledge alone would release her to make a freer choice. When the Tarot shows us some subconscious pattern the information will sink back again unless we make an effort to change. If the woman had said, 'Now that I know I desire weakness, I can make sure not to do so,' she would have kept it in mind for a while and then forgotten about it, or at least not connected it to her actual behaviour. To help avoid this we worked out a series of meditations for her to do using a pattern formed from the cards. The pattern included Strength right side up as a way for her to develop a more positive relationship to the archetypal idea of strength. The meditations did not guarantee a change. But at least they pushed her to deal with the issues raised by the reading rather than assume she had overcome the problems just by learning about them.

The actual reading showed an undesirable result in the relationship between the outcome and the possible outcome. Some people seeing this would believe they were trapped and would have to face the bad news. Others would take the attitude that if they didn't want it they could easily change it. Neither position is true. She could change the result but only through a serious effort. The reading demonstrated the way things were headed. It laid out some of the longstanding patterns behind the current trend. If she wished to turn this around she would have to break those patterns. The meditation used the images for just that purpose, thereby freeing her will to choose what she wanted.

In this example the reading did not look at the origin of her beliefs about strength and weakness. It might have done so with particular cards, for instance those of parental influence if the ideas came from her mother or father. Instead, the reading deals with the issue in the present. This tells her that she herself need not search through her past. She can look at the problem as it stands now. On the other hand, the last reading in this book — which results in almost exactly the same outcome configuration as the one just mentioned — directs the subject to examine her childhood awe of her father. One of the many things we learn from Tarot readings is the fact that similar problems might require different solutions.

At this point we might take a look at the question of desirable and undesirable results. There are people who will argue that there is no such thing as an undersirable Tarot reading. We must learn to accept reality, and every experience can teach us something. But if the person yearns for something and the reading shows it will not occur or if the person treasures something and the reading shows its loss, then we cannot call this desirable. And if the reading indicates the person can avoid this outcome then we should help him or her to do so effectively. On the other hand, many readings show a loss or a failure with the suggestion that it can lead to a fresh start or a greater gain. Other readings may show problems but indicate that the struggle will bring joy or liberation. Then the task becomes to help the subject see the benefits and not just the pain.

The examples given above involve, for the most part, consciousness and matters of choice. Therefore, we can talk of alternatives and free will. Sometimes, however, a reading will show something unpleasant that cannot be avoided, because the subject is not the primary agent bringing it about. It may come from the decisions of other people who refuse to be swayed. In that case the reader can look at the subject's probable response and help her or him to get through the situation.

If Tarot readings concern such matters as changing consciousness or uncovering repressed patterns and expectations, does that make them a kind of psychotherapy? Some time ago I talked about this with a therapist, a former student of mine who uses the cards in her sessions. She told me how she would sometimes do a conventional reading but more often would tell the person to choose some cards and then would say, 'Tell me a story about these pictures.' Depending on what the client said she would then help him or her to relate these to the ongoing concerns of the therapy. Though the Tarot may help break down blocks or open new areas, it serves primarily to initiate something beyond itself. The way to that something comes from the client's responses to the cards, not from the therapist's interpretations.

In the kind of reading in this book the focus remains on the cards. The reader is responsible for interpreting them. This does not mean ignoring the subject. If the reader suggests a particular meaning for a card and the subject says, 'No, that doesn't seem right to me,' then of course the reader must respect this. More subtly, the reader needs to notice when something strikes home and when something seems to miss. Sometimes this becomes obvious, and no one needs to say anything. Once, in a workshop, I asked for a volunteer to do a demonstration reading. I made it clear that the reading might show something personal, and the person must be willing for the others to see whatever comes up. (I should take the opportunity to say that all the subjects whose readings appear in this book gave their permission at the time of the reading.) When we laid out the cards they described some kind of heartbreak and I began to talk about the experience in terms of the images. Afterwards, one of the other members in the workshop asked how I could speak with such assurance about someone I had never met before that morning. I answered that I was reading the cards, and the cards made clear their message. I did not say that the woman herself made clear the truth of the interpretation by beginning to cry (very quietly, so that no one noticed but myself sitting next to her) almost as soon as we began the discussion.

And yet, the reply was correct. For unlike the therapist, who uses the image as a jumping off point, the reader must always return to the cards. The reader's primary task is to provide information. And that information comes from the reader's understanding of and sensitivity to the symbols. The therapist works in an ongoing situation with many factors such as the client's detailed accounts of personal history. The reader works with the cards. In describing these readings I have tended to give minimal information about the people involved. Now and then I have stated the value of knowing certain factors ahead of time. But too much outside knowledge can swamp the reader and draw him or her away from the pictures. Even if we know the person intimately we should attempt at first to look at the reading in the same way we would look at a reading done for a stranger. Then, as the cards raise certain issues we can allow our knowledge of the person to deepen the interpretations. But we must always return to the cards, for in doing so we allow the Tarot to perform its special function, that of telling us things we do not already know.

If the cards appear to say something that contradicts what you think you know about the person, give the cards a chance. Try out the idea and see where it leads. If it leads nowhere, if the subject does not respond with anything more than a shrug or a confused look then try something else. But never rule out an interpretation because your conscious appraisal tells you otherwise. We do Tarot readings precisely because they bring us information from a source beyond our conscious arrangement of the world. Several times I have seen readings that made no sense at all according to what I knew of the person and the situation, but as soon as I began to explain it the subject made it clear that the reading described something very real. At other times the subject has told me that the reading did not apply, and because the cards spoke so clearly I have kept with the interpretations, only to have the subject tell me some time later that life surprised her or him by working out the way the cards had suggested. (Some people might think the reading acts as a self-fulfilling prophecy, causing the person to act in a particular way because of the predictions. In my experience this idea assigns too much power to the cards and the reader. One of the valuable lessons we learn from Tarot readings is the difficulty of altering the direction of a person's behaviour. People tend to do what they are going to do.)

So the readings differ from therapy in keeping their primary focus on the symbols. They differ as well in their somewhat more limited possibilities for creating change. I have stressed here and elsewhere that the value of a reading depends on what the person does with it, that the reader should try to point out the ways in which the person can use the images to move the situation in beneficial ways. Several of the readings in this book emphasize the choices open to the person or the way the reading shows one particular way of dealing with the problems. Two of the readings are followed by a short series of meditations using cards from the readings. Nevertheless, a Tarot reading is usually a one-time event, even if the person might return at some later date. It lacks therapy's continuing framework for energizing growth and new behaviour.

Several of the readings in this book come from people who have done or continue to do a series of readings with me. These readings serve as signposts in their developments, both in the sense of keeping them on track and sending them in new directions. By seeing which themes, and especially which cards, continue to appear, they can discover what has changed, what remains the same, and what they have done and become in the times between readings. In one reading seen here the Magician reversed appears as the woman's past experience. A pessimistic image, it made the woman aware of a certain pattern of weakness and blocked potentials. The awareness helped her to work on these problems so that in her following reading the Magician reversed appeared not in the past but as one of her 'work cards' in the present.

In a series of readings a specific card might take on personal meaning. The king of Cups might signify artistic ambition, the ten of Wands a pattern of behaviour in a relationship. By doing a series they give the cards greater dimension and themselves greater possibilities for using the symbols for change. But even in these cases the particular readings will usually take place anywhere from two to three weeks to six months apart. One man returns once every two or three years. A woman does a reading with me once a year. Because her situation has not fundamentally changed in the last few years several of the same cards have shown up in almost every reading.

The reader owes it to the subject to interpret the cards as best as he or she can, gleaning understanding from the symbols and showing how the person can use them. The decision of what to do with the reading will always remain with the subject. This is another reason for returning to the images. The power of divination will come through them and that power can leave its mark on the subject, hopefully prodding her or him to new perceptions and understandings. If the person desires change then the cards can help, even push for it; if not, the subject will go away, impressed or unimpressed by the information gained, and eventually the reading will fade from the mind.

This situation sometimes produces a feeling of frustration for the reader who sees the message clearly, sees the potentials and wants the subject to pursue them, yet knows it will not happen. A man came to me once with a problem that had gone on for a long time. Several years before the reading he had begun to develop psychic abilities, especially clairvoyance. His experience had so unnerved him that he eventually suffered a nervous breakdown. Though he had left the hospital he continued to take tranquillizers to suppress these experiences and his anxiety about them. He wanted to know what he could do. When we laid the cards a very strong message came through. The cards told him he could get through this crisis, he could learn to direct his powers so they would feed his life instead of destroying it. But he needed a teacher, someone who had gone this way before and could direct him through the traps. Without a teacher to act as an anchor he would continue to lose himself in fear and confusion. This information shone as clearly as any I've ever seen, and I offered to send him to a couple of teachers I knew who could either help him themselves, or else direct him further. But he could not listen. A clairvoyant himself, and very frightened, he needed to hear it from a psychic. He feared to accept advice from someone whose knowledge was not outright, not absolute.

The psychic reader uses the Tarot as a stimulant for inner revelations. The cards serve a function similar to that of a photograph or a piece of jewellery for a psychometrist. The non-psychic reader who wishes to predict will usually depend on a series of formulae, some of them specific almost to the point of absurdity. One text advises that if a certain card appears beside another, 'You will go on a picnic but you will have to leave early because of rain.' I once witnessed a reading done with this text and the cards that go with it. To my amazement the two cards appeared. The reader interpreted the 'picnic' metaphorically.

There is much evidence that the literal style of divination (rather than the psychic or the symbolic) formed the most common approach in ancient times. Archaeologists have uncovered lists of predictions belonging to particular configurations in some divinatory system. The ancient Chinese burned tortoiseshells until they cracked open, then interpreted the shapes of the cracks. The Babylonians poured oil onto a bowl of water and watched where the bubbles formed. In both cases the meanings came from a list of specific descriptions.

As soon as we begin to interpret the Tarot symbolically rather than literally we discover the need for a personal relationship with the cards. Symbolic interpretation allows a whole range of possible interpretations, and while we can learn at least some of these from texts, others will emerge only in practice. By entering the images we create meanings as we go along. With such a variety of meanings it becomes necessary to choose which ones apply in any particular reading. The king of Pentacles might represent the subject or the subject's husband or a business associate. If herself, it might signify her ambitions, or her limitations, or her fixed ideas, or her 'masculine' side, and so on. To determine what it means requires an intense feeling for the symbols. 'Staying with the image' means we must love the image.

This idea of choice does not mean only one meaning can apply in any reading. As we go through these examples we will find again and again that symbolic interpretation allows any number of possibilities for a single card, some of them apparently contradictory. Our logic-bound culture leads us to assume that if a person holds a particular attitude, say a desire to free himself from a certain situation, then he cannot at the same time cling to the situation. But the psyche follows a different kind of logic in which things very often call up their opposites rather than exclude them. A symbol can stand for several different things at once, and the interpretation of a Tarot card does not lie in any single meaning but in the complex of meanings. The different aspects of the symbol feed each other, they give each other energy, increasing the potency of the symbol to affect our lives.

In his 'structuralist' method of interpreting myth, Claude Lévi-Strauss advocates using all versions of a story, no matter how far flung, (including, for instance, Freud's Oedipus complex along with Sophocles' Oedipus plays). In the same way, the 'meaning' of a Tarot card lies in the play between all its possible interpretations. This includes future interpretations as well as past, for a Tarot card, like a myth, is never explained away. New understandings, new discoveries always lie ahead.

And yet, this sum of all meanings will not apply in a specific reading. Yes, we need to look at different interpretations, even seeking out contradictory ones, and yes, we should not restrict ourselves or try to resolve the various aspects into one, but this does not mean we should put in everything ever encountered or conceivable about a card without discrimination. For if the Tarot as a whole is like a myth, then a specific reading is more like a dream, highly personal and immediate. Therefore, the reader must seek those meanings which lead us into the labyrinth of this reading, this dream. In *Seventy-Eight Degrees of Wisdom, Part Two* I described certain Minor Arcana cards as 'gate cards' and suggested somewhat esoteric uses for their images. Three of those cards — the ten, the six, and the nine of Pentacles — appear in the next to last reading in this book. And yet, despite all three coming from the same suit, the interpretations only invoke the 'hidden' qualities for one of these cards, the six. I could give a 'logical' explanation for this, by saying that I make it a rule to avoid esoteric associations unless the reading seems to insist on it, and that this occurred with the six (its gate symbolism relates it to Justice, and Justice lay beside it in the reading); but in fact, the decision did not follow any fixed rules. It came out of my response to the cards in their context.

In considering the interpretation of dreams many people assume everything stands for something else according to a definite programme. Elongated objects always signify penises, flying always represents sexual desire, and so on. While some analysts no doubt work this way, many others discourage such assumptions and push the dreamer to approach the dream through response. If a man dreams about a stick, never mind the phallic association, what does this stick mean to him? Similarly, the Tarot reader must always rely on his or her feeling about the cards. However much we have learned, a Tarot reading always takes us back to the intuitive. The centre of the labyrinth is the unconscious, whose formlessness defeats all our attempts to map or limit it.

The choices shown here are necessarily my choices, based on my knowledge of the cards and my feeling for the way they come together in each reading. In some cases, the explanation will expand the possible meanings, in others the same card may receive a relatively narrow interpretation. Whatever logical basis the commentary possesses it originates in reactions to the pictures.

Because Tarot readings, like dreams, are personal, they uncover new meanings and values for the old images. Because they are not only personal they carry the acquired meanings with them to be used in future readings. Various interpretations discussed in this book originally came out of past readings.

The Tarot images form a world, one that mirrors and gives order to the outside world of lives and events. Whatever their origin the cards have developed, over the centuries, into an eloquent and suggestive depiction of the soul's experience in life. When we lay out a Tarot reading we create a context for the individual. Ultimately this is what a Tarot reading does. It sets the person in a context of past experience, future trends, current forces. And because of the non-personal side of the symbols a reading sets the subject in an archetypal context as well.

By 'archetypes' I mean images that express a complex of human experience — think of the Empress with all its symbolism to create the image of passion and nature — and at the same time carry a sense of meaning greater than we can ever define. In this usage it does not matter so much whether or not the images occur spontaneously to people in different cultures at different times — the usual definition of the term. What matters is what the image evokes in us. Because an archetype is a constellation out of the unconscious, it produces a sense of yearning, or reaching for an ultimate understanding that always recedes from us the more we expand and explain it. Consider the Fool and his leap from the mountaintop. We can define this in terms of innocence, or freedom, or the spirit's incarnation into mortality. But in fact no definition will ever pin down the joy and awe created by contemplating the image.

And yet, the explanations are not empty or trivial. Part of the power of the archetypes lies in its ability to generate ideas. The unconsciousness feeds consciousness by creating images and concepts for consciousness to consider. Through wrestling with meaning, the mind exercises itself and becomes stronger. And so feeds energy back to the image. A creative tension exists between the mystery and its interpretations. In the Tarot, mountains signify the concept of abstract truth. But they are also mountains as well, with all the ancient associations related to human experience with peaks. The greater the web of symbolic meaning the more the image draws us down to its ultimate mystery.

We often think of archetypes as transcending human nature, as if human nature consisted only of the transitory aspects of daily life. But in fact archetypes *are* human nature, they generate the most essential human quality, the ability to move between current experience and an awareness of eternity.

We also think of archetypes as transcending history, unchanging, independent of culture and events. But in fact archetypes are history itself. They embody humanity's spiritual history in the form of images.

Those images arise out of our continual attempts to conceptualize
the world without falsifying it. The Hanged Man gains much of its
power from the age of the symbol. Nor do archetypes stand outside
of culture. In the card of the Lovers we see the man look to the woman
while the woman looks to the angel. The scene implies that rationality
can take us only so far and then must yield to the unconscious. We
find God through mystery and not reason. Now, this idea, and the
symbolism that expresses it, reverses the historic teaching of
Christianity, which directed women to look to their husbands for
spiritual guidance since men followed intellect and women emotions.
The Tarot trump takes the cultural assumption and turns it around.
We think of archetypes as transcending history because they arise
from such deep roots in history itself.

A Tarot reading sets a person in a context of history: personal
history, cultural history, spiritual history. Even while it outlines the
immediate condition it connects her or him to something vast and
unknowable. And yet, despite its archetypal openings, a reading
remains immediate. The images describe this person, now. Probably
at different times in a person's life all the archetypes of the Tarot will
apply. At any single time, however, the cards show us which symbols
represent our experience. They say that right now you are the High
Priestess, silent and private, or the joyous child of the Sun, or the
woman who sits shrouded in her boat carrying her six Swords. At
some future date the archetypes will shift, you will become a different
person and different symbols will describe you. For now, you are
this person, with these images.

We tend to think of personality as a single structure. One person,
always the same within, whatever the outer manifestations. This belief
in an inner unchangeable self possibly derives from our monotheistic
tradition. The idea of one God ruling the universe leads us to think
of ourselves as one essential being. But perhaps we would find it more
useful if we saw ourselves as many different people over the course
of our lives. The current interest in polytheistic religions — Hindu,
American Indian, Voodoo, even the ancient Greek and Norse
pantheons — derives partly from a rebellion against the monotheistic
view of personality. Worshippers of Voodoo see themselves as under
the influence of different gods at different times. The psychologist
James Hillman writes of using the Greek gods and goddesses to
'personify' our experiences.

As a system (not just a collection) of archetypes, the Tarot allows
us to personify shifting personalities in terms of concrete images. And
a reading will show which ones apply at specific times. We should

avoid, however, any idea that the cards control us. We may say, almost for the sake of convenience, 'I need to keep to myself for a while, I'm under the influence of the Hermit,' or even 'Justice is ruling me,' but we should remember that the images are not beings who take over our lives.

And yet, we can use these archetypes almost as if they were living creatures, to move our lives in desired ways. In the two readings using meditation, each person deliberately sought identification with the queen of Cups. They saw the card as the embodiment of what they wished to become. In the first Celtic cross reading Justice so represented the subject's deepest sense of himself that the card became his personal archetype, signifying his yearning to express intellect as the bringer of spirit into the world. In such moments a Tarot reading does more than give information. It gives us ourselves.

TWO NOTES ON TERMS

1. Throughout this book I have used the expression 'subject' to designate the person for whom the cards are laid. The word is not wholly satisfactory. It suggests a slightly clinical approach. On the other hand I find the traditional 'querent' too quaint, and 'client' somehow carries associations of an ad agency (despite its use by many psychotherapists).

2. Ever since psychoanalysis first focused attention on non-conscious experience, people have tended to use the terms 'subconscious' and 'unconscious' as synonyms. This book, like *Seventy-Eight Degrees of Wisdom Part Two* makes a sharp distinction between the two words. By 'subconscious' I mean desires, fears, rages, and so on that the conscious mind represses in its awareness of itself. This material belongs to the ego (or perhaps becomes attached to it) for it originates in experiences the ego does not wish to acknowledge but cannot eradicate.

   'Unconscious' evokes the basic energy of life, formless, unending, connecting us to the universe. We do not know it directly, but only through its images, the archetypes and myths which surge up into consciousness.

Chapter 1.

A Three Card Reading

Three card readings are not very common in Tarot divination. For one thing, they are simply too short. There are less cards individually to work with, and less combinations are possible than if, say, ten or twenty-one cards are involved. They are also less structured. In the larger readings each position has a meaning, such as 'basis' or 'past experience' and that meaning gives the reader a place to start in considering the card. But with only three it is more difficult to be precise. We can call them past, present, future, or else self, situation, other people, but these are such broad categories to assign to such few cards.

Sometimes people will use three cards for a simple yes or no answer to a direct question. One Tarot reader I've met told me that she asks the question and turns over three cards. If two or three are right side up the answer is yes; if upside down, then no. You can try, as an experiment, asking a series of simple yes or no questions over a period of days and checking the answers against events. I admit that I have not done so, and for much the same reason that I do not use the cards in general for yes/no questions. My own approach ('bias' might be a better word) leads me to look at the more complex meanings whenever I lay the cards out in any form, so that my attempt to see only the number of rightside up cards becomes sabotaged by the pattern that emerges from the three together. And as long as a pattern is involved it might as well be a larger one.

However, three cards, by their very brevity, can sometimes succinctly describe a situation. If the 'moment' is right, if that click happens to open up the unconscious, then a three card reading can emerge with much wider meaning than we would normally expect.

The following reading occurred by accident. I had gone to visit a friend who was also a therapist (the woman mentioned in the introduction). When I arrived she had just finished a weekly session with a group who had been meeting with her for years. I had known them myself, through my friend, for several years, and at one time or another in the past had read the cards for all of them. In their sessions they would sometimes use the Tarot to trigger responses or to get themselves to confront what was happening in their lives. When I arrived that night they had been turning over cards, but more in a spirit of half-serious play (a Foolish spirit) than real searching. One of the women pointed to three cards before her and asked me what I thought about them. The cards were:

The reading showed her at a kind of focal point in her life, where she could go in either of two directions. The Devil represented sinking into weakness, obsession, a feeling of being trapped without any control over the direction or circumstances of her life. From a previous reading I knew that in the past a difficult situation had brought out such Devil attitudes in her (though I knew nothing about the facts of her current situation, later conversation indicated that she was struggling with some of the same problems). At that time she had disliked the structure of her life but felt powerless, for practical and emotional reasons, to change it. Therefore, it seemed to me that the page of Cups represented an attempt to detach herself from the Devil's illusion of helplessness, while Temperance signified the possibility, not just of change, but of becoming more in control. Reflective, the page of Cups looks calmly at whatever arises from pondering the situation. Therefore, it suggests her work in therapy, and her general attempt to separate herself from the obsessiveness represented by the Devil. For the Devil signifies illusions. The chains are wide enough to slip over the neck. That which traps the demons is their belief that they are trapped — their willingness to accept the situation because it's easier to do nothing and to stay unhappy or dissatisfied than to attempt a change. The first step, then, is detachment. Not action, but separation, for without detachment, action, at least productive action, remains impossible. She would simply run about without removing the chains.

She needed to look at her life and herself with an honesty that comes from not pressuring herself to do anything. The page of Cups signifies this attitude, for in contrast to the knight, who tries to withdraw but feels the pressure of responsibility, the page, symbolically a child, allows himself just to look at things.

The fish symbolizes the imagination and therefore the page does not simply look at things already known but allows the unknown to emerge. He lets himself reflect on whatever comes up. The Devil suppresses possibilities, not only of change, but even of imagination, perhaps especially of imagination. We feel trapped when we believe the illusory message: what you see now is all there is. Therefore, the page of Cups performs a great service by freeing the mind as the first step to freeing the body.

Here we find one of the values of doing Tarot readings. Who would think that so modest a card as the page of Cups could serve as antidote to the entrapments of the Devil? Yet, by seeing the two of them side-by-side, and by reflecting on them in exactly that page of Cups aspect, we discover that the page of Cups is just what is needed. Thus a reading brings a new combination into being, one that resides from now on in the store of knowledge, to be drawn on for future work, whether in divination, study, meditation, or exercises. Knowledge once created remains. And only a reading could have created it, by bringing the two images into conjunction. At the start of the discussion with the group someone asked if I ever learned anything new from the cards. The relation between the Devil and the page of Cups is an example of such new knowledge.

Temperance represents the alternative to the Devil. Where the Devil is extreme, Temperance is moderate. Where the Devil is obsessive, Temperance is calm, realistic. Temperance is balanced, above all in control compared to the Devil's feeling of something controlling you from outside.

How, then, to get to Temperance from the page of Cups? For the page, despite the withdrawal from the Devil's traps, remains passive, and in fact, his ability to ponder and reflect depends on that passivity. As soon as action is called for there is a danger of losing detachment, of falling into the same old traps. Therefore, she needs a bridge from the one state to the other. The solution lies partly in the symbolism of the cups. Where the page holds one, the angel of Temperance holds two and pours the water between them. In some decks the two cups are gold and silver, the solar and lunar principles of action and reflection. In other words, the trick is to keep that spirit of detached contemplation in the midst of action. Quite a 'trick' of course; easy to recommend and difficult to accomplish. The picture gives us an added hint. The angel does not hold the cups separately but pours the water from one to the other. We do not remain detached by isolating the observing aspect from the events and decisions of daily life. Such an approach breeds the neurotic feeling of being cut off from everything you do. In a way it returns you to the Devil, for under the influence of that card, you go through life with the sense that an outside force has control of you and nothing you do yourself can make any real difference. Temperance, on the other hand, gives us a portrait of autonomy.

In Temperance observation blends with action. The two become inseparable. The reflective self asks questions. What is really happening here? Just what am I doing and why am I doing it? How did this situation develop? These questions have meaning because they refer to decisions and concrete steps. And these steps come from the recognition that change and development in your life depends on you.

The card of the Devil shows two people under the Devil's control. Moreover, in the Rider-Waite pack (the deck used in these readings) the card appears as a parody of the Lovers (the Devil is 15, 1 + 5 = 6, the number of the Lovers).

The situation that had led the woman to feel trapped was a complex double relationship. The exact structure of that involvement is not important here. What matters is that it led to the loss of autonomy.

And now notice that the two cards after the Devil contain only one figure each. Through the page of Cups we see the necessity that she pull back from the situation in order to reflect on it and on her own choices. This means pulling back from the other people as well. In Temperance we see that in action as well she must learn to rely on herself, not the others. She must make her own decisions and act on them as best she can.

It might be argued that this is good advice at any time, and therefore Temperance's appearance here does not tell her anything she wouldn't already know. To regard the card simply as advice, however, is to miss the point. For in this reading Temperance does not simply advise (as it does sometimes in other readings) but declares that such a way of being has become possible. The reading tells her that the time has come to begin to live autonomously, not just to look at her problems, as in the page of Cups, but begin to solve them. Therefore, Temperance is not only a recommendation, but a challenge. She can leave the Devil behind — if she chooses.

In the task of developing autonomy, the card of Temperance serves as aid as well as description. The card is not an intellectual account of what's needed, but a printed picture, a symbol you can hold in your hand. You can ponder the image or allow it to work on you at a non-conscious level. You can meditate with it, or carry it around, to have a sense of it with you, or even press it against your body, feeling the force of the symbol opening up areas of blocked energy.

To people raised in an intellectual tradition such suggestions may sound faintly idolatrous, or just silly. The only answer to these objections is that it works. In reaching beyond mental acceptance of an idea to actual practice, we should not underestimate the use of Tarot cards as concrete symbols. At the same time, the proper use of symbols begins with intellectual comprehension. We must understand what the card means before we try to assimilate that meaning, for the card only represents the truth embodied in the symbol. And in fact the mind-work never stops. When you bring the picture into yourself and yourself into the picture, you find that fresh insights bubble up at you, not just about the symbol, but about your own life, and about how the symbol and what it represents can work in your life.

On the question of the particular recommendations made by Temperance, we should also realize that other cards might have appeared with equal force but with very different meanings. The Fool would have suggested a very different path to release from the Devil. And the Lovers would have urged her to trust to her primary relationship to give her strength, rather than to seek it within herself. In connection with the Devil on the other side of the page of Cups, the Lovers would have told her to correct her perceptions about what the relationship offered her. But the card does not appear. Temperance comes instead, with its special message of balance and rational action.

Finally, in regard to the approach to a symbol, it is not only Temperance the woman needs to ponder in this way, but also the Devil. For even if the page of Cups indicates that she has reflected on the situation, the appearance of the trump suggests that the Devil has not faded into the past. As a real danger — and temptation — in the present it requires a full understanding of its reality in order for her to escape it.

Above we saw that she can leave the Devil behind if she chooses, and that Temptation was challenging her. This brings us to the idea that the page of Cups shows her at a pivotal point, with the possibility for going either way, to the Devil, or to Temperance. The movement to autonomy is not a natural evolution. It does not simply happen. She must make it happen through a conscious choice and effort.

The Devil holds a great attraction. With chains comes the removal of responsibility. You can always blame the other people, or the situation itself. There is nothing you have to do if there's nothing you can do. Always remember that the imprisoned figures appear at ease, comfortable. And the Devil is exciting. It produces wild swings of emotion. It goes to extremes. Many people beginning to work with the Tarot find Temperance boring. What they seek in life and therefore in the Tarot is excitement, and a prescription to walk the middle way and do everything in moderation seems the opposite of that intense charge they hope to get from spiritual exploration. Indeed, some people find themselves drawn to the Devil because of its connotations of 'black magic' and forbidden rites. But the figure on the card of Temperance is an angel, a being of great power and radiance. This is precisely the lesson we must learn from the card, that autonomy is worth achieving, and not simply because it's safer, or provides material benefits, or because it's worth giving up the highs in order to get rid of the lows. Temperance signifies a joy that goes beyond momentary thrills. It symbolizes a direct connection to the unconscious which is the source of life, a connection both developed and expressed through the practice of moderation. People find Temperance boring because they see it as caution, or a self control that doesn't dare to take any chances. We can call this 'fake Temperance' imposed by repression or fear (we sometimes see this fake Temperance in readings as the trump upside down). The angel on the card does not symbolize timidity.

The reading shows the woman poised between the two possibilities: forward to Temperance or a slide back to the Devil. We must consider then, what sort of base the page of Cups provides for making the beneficial but difficult choice. And here we run into difficulties. For while the childlike qualities of the page allow the freedom to reflect without responsibility, the call to Temperance has now come upon her, and she must recognize the need to give up the page of Cups as well as the Devil. Powerlessness links the two cards — in the Devil because of control from outside, in the page because of the sense of being a child who does not need to do anything but only to look. The angel on the other hand is a being of power, and so the reading was telling the woman that her belief in her own weakness was no longer valid. She may cling to it but it is not true. Temperance has become appropriate to her life now. But she must take up the challenge. It cannot just happen. To remain passive would invite a slide back to the Devil. That too would be her choice.

After we had discussed these aspects of the reading, a different way of looking at it came into my mind. Instead of seeing it as a crisis of the moment we could consider it as a general pattern in her life. At times she thought of herself as helpless and enslaved by circumstances and her own weakness. At other times she found herself in control, making positive changes, avoiding violent mood swings. In each condition, the Devil or Temperance, that one appeared real and the other appeared as a fantasy. While under the Devil's influence she found the problems insurmountable. The idea that she could ever control her life seemed a sad illusion. But then she would take some positive steps, get out of her depression, act on the insights gained in therapy. At such moments she would consider herself free of that helpless state. She would believe, 'This is the real me.' Until the next time.

If she could slide backwards like that, did that invalidate those times of feeling free? Were they fake Temperance? It seemed to me that the cards said the opposite. The moments in control were real, though perhaps they gave more of a taste of autonomy than the full realization of it. The illusion came when she thought she had broken free once and for all. And so, when she met obstacles, it became easy to fall back again.

In this interpretation the page of Cups represented the ability to detach herself from both experiences, to look calmly at them, and thereby recognize their reality and their limits. In this way she could begin to work towards emerging from the cycle.

The reading shows us something fresh about the relation of

Temperance to the Devil. The two cards appear side-by-side in the Major Arcana, where their numbers are 14 and 15. Notice that Temperance comes first. If we divide the trumps into three rows of seven (setting the Fool aside as having no number, and therefore no fixed place) we see that Temperance culminates the second line and therefore symbolizes a kind of victory over the self. The question then arises as to why the Devil can appear directly after this victory. In my book on the Major Arcana, *Seventy-Eight Degrees of Wisdom, Part One* I suggested certain answers to this question. This reading implies another. Temperance does not just form the end of one sequence and the Devil the beginning of another. The two exist side-by-side and they form a kind of intimate relationship in which each one represents half of a reality. By themselves, each of those halves is an illusion. Only by accepting both sides of ourselves, the times when we feel confident and in control of the direction of our lives, and the times in which we once again fall into weakness, obsession and pain, can we understand who we are. And only by taking a step backward to look calmly at the cycle, in the manner of the page of Cups, can we understand and perhaps begin to work our way out of it.

One final point needs our attention. We have looked at several interpretations of these three cards, some of which might seem mutually exclusive, so that the question arises, which one is the truth? In fact, they are all true. The woman was both at a pivotal point in her life where she had to make decisions and act on them, *and* she tended to follow a pattern of helplessness/responsibility. Readings often will produce varying meanings, all of them correct. The fullest interpretation lies in the mosaic formed by the different ways of looking at the images and their relationships.

And something else; even if a particular interpretation should not apply to the subject's life at that moment it still remains valid. For Tarot readings do not exist only for their subjects. Every Tarot reading can teach us something about the world, and while the reader's first responsibility remains that of making it meaningful for the person who mixed the cards, the reader should also look beyond that situation to see the wider truths that may emerge from pondering the situation.

Chapter 2.

The Celtic Cross

Over the years the Celtic cross has become the most popular 'spread' for laying out the cards. No doubt this derives partly from the fact that Arthur Waite, designer of the Rider pack, recommended it in his own book, so that subsequent writers using Waite's deck have also included the cross in their descriptions. But the spread's popularity arises also from its great value as a tool of knowledge. It consists of ten positions, each of which tells something by itself, but which together evoke valuable combinations and relationships.

In *Seventy-Eight Degrees of Wisdom, Part Two* I gave a detailed description of the positions in the Celtic cross and their possible interpretations. Since these possibilities will become clear through the examples that follow, a simple outline should give us an idea of the cross's construction. The pattern looks like this:

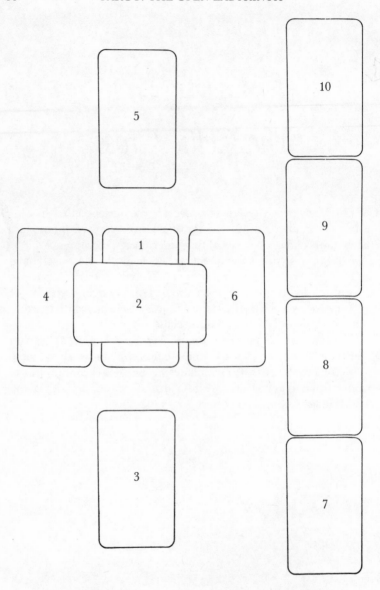

The positions are as follows.

1. The centre. This card (plus the second) outlines the essential situation examined in the reading. It shows something that lies at the core of the complex formed in the other cards.

2. The crossing card. Some books describe this position as an opposition to the first, or to the subject her/himself. I have found it useful to look at it as a complement to the centre, and sometimes as a development arising out of the central situation.

3. The basis. This position looks behind the central issues to the question of roots and causes. It usually shows past experience, but can sometimes indicate a current development.

4. The recent past. The card indicates an experience that has contributed to the general situation. The experience may have ended, in which case its influence remains for now, or else it continues into the present, but temporarily. Either way, it forms a more transitory influence than that of the basis.

5. The possible outcome. One of the most important positions, and for many readers one of the most difficult to interpret. It shows, first of all, a potential development, a trend in which the reading is headed, but one that lacks the solidity of the final card, the outcome, or of the more definite (but more limited) 'near future'. Sometimes the possible outcome derives from the outcome as a further unfolding. At other times it may appear to contradict the outcome and shows an alternative development that will not actually take place. If the possible appears desirable the subject may wish to use it as a goal and consider how to bring it about. If undesirable, then she or he may consider what steps to take to avoid it.

6. The near future. More limited than the previous card, this position shows some influence that will soon affect the subject. Though important, and often a contribution to the outcome, the specific situation is not likely to last. This transitory aspect can often be important to remember. If it's good, make the most of it. If a problem, remember that it will pass.

The final four cards form what is known as the 'staff'. They show various elements contributing to the pattern.

7. Self. Not the whole person, but some attitude or activity that affects the situation.

8. Environment. This position can refer to specific people and their effect on the person, or it can mean the general environment in which the subject finds her/himself. What matters most (as with the card of self) is the contribution to the overall development.

9. Hopes and fears. Another vital card, because it shows what the person expects from the situation. We should avoid looking at it simplistically, i.e. a good image means something hoped for,

a bad means something feared. Often, what the conscious mind recognizes as beneficial the subconscious will shun. The subconscious is conservative and hates change. Similarly, something undesirable to consciousness may attract the subconscious as a way of protecting itself.

10. The outcome. While this card 'predicts' in the sense of showing the likely result of the different trends and influences, we should not read it in isolation, but as the summation of all the others. It does not represent anything fixed or unalterable, but shows the way things are heading. By using the information gained in the reading the subject can work to change the situation. Still, the change may not come easily, especially if the influences come from deep roots. Avoidance of a difficult outcome may require a great effort.

CELTIC CROSS ONE

The following reading was done for a twenty-nine year old man who could not seem to find a direction for himself. He had moved to Europe from the United States in order to live with a lover, but the relationship had fallen apart. He had studied history and philosophy and felt a passionate connection to these subjects, yet had not found a way to make a career from his interests. He had worked at journalism, though he considered himself only a beginner as a professional. Finally he had tried creative writing, and liked the results, but did not know if his work was good enough to pursue or was likely to sell.

The reading did not address any of these specific issues. Instead, it looked at his life overall, showing a current crisis of development and the possibility of emerging from it. We chose the knight of Cups as the significator, the knight because he had not found his direction in life, and Cups because of his artistic interests and an introspective quality in his character that matched the card. The cards came out as shown opposite.

We began our interpretation with a general overview. The reading shows blocked potentials. The three of Pentacles indicates the possibility of artistic and professional mastery, but reversed shows it likely not to emerge under the current influences. Similarly, the Star reversed indicates a kind of despair rising from a sense that life *could* open up, bringing joy and confidence — but wasn't doing so. Judgement suggested a crucial time, in which he should rise to a new level, leaving old problems and configurations behind. But that too did not happen. The key seemed to lie in Justice reversed. Before that card in the basis position the reading showed two right side up cards. From Justice

on the cards all came out upside down. The lack of Justice at the root prevented the other possibilities from fulfilling themselves.

The Knight of Wands

We then went on to look at the individual cards. The first, the knight of Wands, showed a quality almost opposite from that of the significator. Where the knight of Cups sits quietly on his horse, the Wands' knight charges ahead. Where Cups looks inward, resisting all tugs from outside, Wands directs his attention on the world and its temptations. Thus the card shows him moving away from introspection to action. But we shall see that introspection is what he needs. Because of this need, the action lacks direction and purpose. Wands is the suit of beginnings, of formless fire energy. It requires clear goals and plans, it requires a firm foundation for the energy not to burn itself out. Notice that the knight rides through a desert, devoid of houses and people as well as trees and water. Without something to carry that energy to a purpose, the desert will not open up to life.

But the centre card does not only describe current activity without direction. In this position the knight of Wands depicts some essential issue in the subject's life at the time. Remember that he had spent years moving from one thing to another, trying different kinds of work, entering relationsips, all without yielding any firm ground for his abilities or hopes. Through Judgement, and through the potential qualities of all those other upside-down cards we see that he stands now at the verge of ending that aimless period. In order for that to happen, however, he must find a means to deal with past weaknesses.

Because it does not lead to anything definite, the knight of Wands represents a desire. He wants to do things, to look outside himself, to travel and have adventures. But if such desires derive from escapism, that is, the need to escape the self and its history, then we see the result pictured here, where the necessary qualities, shown in Justice, or the ace of Swords, become unmanageable. The ace of Swords upside-down indicates he has lost control of those qualities symbolized by the card.

Instead of freedom, the flight shown in the knight of Wands results (in this reading) in the repression and bound feelings symbolized as the outcome. The whole reading bursts with potential, the three of Pentacles for mastery, the Star for joy and openness, the ace of Swords for wisdom and intellect, and of course Judgement for the rise of the new self. But none of these actually happen. One key reason for this frustration appears in the knight's desire to get away. Only one other

Wands card, the eight, appears in the reading, and that card when reversed signifies frustration, action without goal or end. Therefore, the Wands energy, often so useful, dissipates itself, and in the near future (the position of the eight).

The knight of Wands does not necessarily mean escapism, or energy which leads nowhere. In fact, the card usually represents some of the suit's most valuable qualities — eagerness, optimism, daring. It is only the context that changes it to frustration. With so many cards calling for self-examination and truth (Justice, the ace, the nine of Cups reversed, Temperance) the movement from the knight of Cups into the knight of Wands signals a flight from dealing with the self.

Judgement

The crossing card, Judgement, indicated the importance of this time in his life. For Judgement symbolizes the possibility of a personal resurrection, in which the subject can shake off old restrictions, old limitations and confusions, and rise from the 'tomb world' of past experiences into a new life. New possibilities will open up, his goals and purposes will become more focused, in general he will experience a feeling of new beginnings, of freedom. Of course, such an experience does not simply happen, but arises from a long development. Yet the causes of that development, even the development itself, may remain hidden from conscious awareness, so that the moment of change appears to occur all at once. Subjectively it may feel as if something stirs the person, something rouses her or him from lethargy and 'summons' him, like the angel Gabriel's trumpet summoning the dead souls to rise out of their graves.

The term 'tomb world' comes from the novelist Philip K. Dick, who used it to indicate a state characterized by alienation, despair, purposelessness, and a sense of life in fragments, none of which fit together. In the forefront of the picture we see a family rising together from their separate tombs. The man and woman represent the opposites of life, the tension between passive and active, between thought and feeling, between hope and reality, between potentiality and being. The gap between the last pair shows through very strongly in this reading. The subject knew his own potentials, artistically, intellectually, professionally, emotionally. And yet, none of these potentials had realized itself.

The child in the picture signifies the union between the poles, just as an actual child is a wholly new being created by the union of his parents. In many earlier trumps, such as the Hierophant or the Lovers, we see the symbol of two people brought together by some uniting power (doctrine in the Hierophant, sexual love in the Lovers). The power keeps the opposites from pulling apart. Here, however, under the influence of the angel's summons, the child emerges between the two. Something new and vital rises out of the ruins of fragmentation. The old shattered life, the tomb world, becomes left behind.

Where does this call come from? Does it originate solely inside the psyche, or from some outside force intervening in our lives to bring solutions and meaning? Sometimes it may result from a long process, in which the person works on himself over a period of time in which nothing seems to come together. Then suddenly, as if something clicks in his life, all the work bears fruit at the same time. Does that click happen only according to some internal laws of the mind? Sometimes a person will make no serious effort, flounder about in life, and yet, for no discernible reason, the change comes, the trumpet sounds, and she or he leaves the tombs behind.

To say that the process goes on unconsciously begs the question. How does it take place without deliberate effort? What triggers the unconscious process, and what makes it suddenly coalesce into an actual transformation?

For people joined to a religious orthodoxy the answers may appear simple. Christ's grace resurrects the fallen being. The penitent returns to Torah. The Goddess saves her child. Yet even simple answers are not necessarily simplistic. Why *this* sinner, or *that* lost child? And for those who do not see the world in terms of a doctrine, the questions posed by Judgement open up the great mysteries of life.

We do Tarot readings to gain information, but in a certain way we do them even more to remind ourselves of our own ignorance. The conscious mind cannot predict how or why Judgement will appear in a person's life. No examination of circumstances, no analysis of the past can give us this knowledge. To see Judgement, or other cards of great significance, appear in a Tarot reading demonstrates the all important limits of rational investigation.

And yet, the recognition of ignorance does not imply that thought or individual effort are useless. Tarot readings show us what we can do as much as what we cannot. We can use that announcement out of the unknown, we can join ourselves to Judgement (or the World, or the Hanged Man, or any of the others) and allow the symbol to carry us forward like a wave. But unless we train our instincts and intellect to accept and comprehend those symbols, their message and purpose will never emerge for us. Even more basic, the recognition of ignorance should not lead to despair at the mind's inability to comprehend everything, but rather to a sense of wonder that such mysteries exist, and that we will never solve all the riddles. If, in the words of the composer Jeanne Lee, 'The miracle is that the layers continue to be stripped away', then equally miraculous is the fact that we can never reach the core. When we compare the materialist smugness of nineteenth-century physics with the awesome uncertainties of quantum theory, we recognize that ignorance, too, is liberation.

If we must acknowledge our ignorance of why Judgement should appear as a force in this person's life at this time we must still look at the question of what it means, and what effect it will have on him. The unsatisfactory developments shown in the other cards would seem to indicate that the call does not lead anywhere or does not connect to anything. But the power of these cards as potentials shows the workings of Judgement. Because of the movement symbolized in Judgement the three of Pentacles and Justice and the ace of Swords all become possible. The real question becomes: what is blocking them from realizing themselves? Why do they all show up reversed?

One answer lies in the relationship between the centre and crossing cards. We have noted above that the second card sometimes emerges from the first. This means that the first will describe a state of being, something essential, while the second will depict the actions or the conscious knowledge that derives from that essential quality. The first, therefore, underpins the second, giving it its base and direction.

In effect, therefore, the knight of Wands and Judgement have come out backwards. Consider the effect if Judgement had occupied the centre and the knight had crossed it. The Wands activity would come from a feeling of new life. The energy would pour from the reborn child. Instead, we see the knight blocking the rebirth. In graphic terms, the knight prevents Judgement from reaching its proper place in the centre of his life. It pushes it outside, to the periphery, where the call still tugs at him, but from a distance, where it cannot break through the barrier he has set up against it. Through activity without purpose and movement without destination he is trying to escape his rebirth.

The next question then becomes, why would anyone run from such a wondrous experience? We must realize firstly that the call only summons, it does not lift the person out of the tomb world by itself. The person must respond. He or she must shrug off the dark waters of past experience in order to rise into the new way of being. And even though that past life has become unsatisfactory it is still safe, if only because the person knows its patterns. Like Temperance (and Temperance reversed — that is, denied — appears in the position that means hopes as well as fears). Judgement challenges us. It does not simply happen, we must make it happen. And to do that requires a recognition of the tomb world itself.

Remember the name of the card — not 'Resurrection' but 'Judgement'. To answer that call requires a recognition of everything that has gone before. We must acknowledge that life has become (or always was) broken apart, without purpose. Before we can make a fresh start we must give up any illusions that things are going well. For many people this appears unbearable. People in terrible marriages will fight any suggestion of divorce because they do not wish to think they have 'wasted' so many years. Middle-aged people with undeveloped talents will refuse opportunities to begin such development by saying 'It's too late for me.' Very often, they really mean, 'I don't want to look at the past.'

In this particular reading, with a younger man who has spent several years living out a false commitment, the fear of Judgement referred more to his immediate experiences of the past years: the love affair gone bad, the many false starts in his search for a direction for his talents and interests. Still, in order to accept Judgement he must understand and accept the past failures.

Justice (reversed)

We see some of these same issues in the card of Justice. The trump — right side up — signifies self-knowledge and a willingness to look honestly at your life, to balance it and determine how it has arrived at this point. Like any true symbol, the picture conveys these ideas through metaphoric images. The primary metaphor for self-examination is sight, so that unlike the legal figure of Justice, this version of the Roman goddess Justitia wears no blindfold but instead stares directly at us. This stare, taken as something from outside, represents the challenge of the card: do we dare to face the truth about our lives? But once we identify with the card, the look becomes our look, and the object changes from ourselves to our actions, our past history, the future that lies before us.

It is worth considering that sight is not the only sense faculty that could have signified examination. Examination may also proceed from touch. A picture of someone touching something to learn about it would have conveyed immediacy and a direct connection to the subject. Sight, on the other hand, suggests distance, a cool detachment that allows us to consider action and consequences without passion and with discrimination, the faculty that distinguishes one thing from another, that carefully separates and judges. The sword provides another metaphor for discrimination. It cuts through dilemmas, it isolates by slicing one thing away from another. Upright, it signifies the pure mind that doesn't lean to one side or the other, but judges honestly and rationally. Only two other cards in the deck bear an upright sword: the ace of Swords and the queen, both of which appear with Justice in this reading. And all three are upside-down, a sign that the subject has lost his purity of thought and very much needs to find a way back to it.

The scales form the third metaphor for examination. In the legal Justice the scales are shown unbalanced, indicating the necessity to decide for one side or the other. Spiritual Justice finds the balance between involvement and reflection, past events and future possibilities, personal actions/decisions and the effects of the outside world. To fully understand ourselves and our history we must give everything its proper weight, looking at it and determining its importance. In older Tarot decks (pre-twentieth century) and in many modern ones, Justice appears as the eighth trump. In this deck, however, it occupies the eleventh position — the exact mid-point of the twenty-one numbered cards. This metaphor of place signifies the still point, the centre from which all movement radiates but which itself remains immobile. That image returns us again to the idea of a dispassionate observer, unmoved by what she sees. The middle position further suggests that whenever we enter into the mood of Justice we have found the mid-point of our lives, no matter what the chronological age. For Justice allows us to see what we have made of ourselves, and where we are going. Above all Justice liberates, for just as awe derives from ignorance, so free will originates in self-knowledge.

All these metaphors — the sword, the cool detachment of the faculty of sight, the balanced scales — suggest the male principle, whose primary attribute is rationality, the ability to separate and make distinctions. Yet the figure of Justice is a woman, and though she raises her sword like the Magician's wand, she sits between two pillars, like the High Priestess, embodiment in the Tarot of the female principle. Thus, Justice implies a unification of opposites. The masculine principle of discrimination leads only to intellectualism unless it operates from an underlying sense of wholeness, from passionate — and instinctive — commitment to truth.

This combination of principles represents the necessary approach to the practice of Tarot readings. Just as we need to define each card's meanings and functions so we need to operate always from a personal attachment to the symbols. And both must derive from a devotion to truth. For this reason I have sometimes described Justice as the patron of divination.

The combination also symbolizes the subject himself, in his feeling for philosophy. While believing in the precision and rationality of the subject he approached it with a personal urgency arising out of love. For him, philosophy was never the intellectual game many people imagine it to be, but rather a carrier and creator of spirit — not truth or knowledge, but spirit itself. Philosophy became a passion because he saw it as the bringer of spiritual power into the world. Through philosophy the mind gave a distinct shape to the formless energy of the unconscious. Philosophy made the mysteries visible. In this reading, therefore, Justice represented not only self-knowledge, not only a commitment to truth, but in fact the subject himself. Justice signified for him a personal archetype, his ideal of what he wanted to become, *and* his best way of dealing with the world.

And Justice was upside-down. The loss of himself indicates a kind of inner disaster and shows us graphically why all the cards after it came out upside-down, as well as why he did not move into the new life opened up in Judgement. The spirit — the angel — is calling him, but he has lost his way of receiving it. Because of his lack of achievement, and because of the draining effect of a bad love affair, he had broken his ties with philosophy. And without that he could do nothing. He could not go forward until he found again his point of beginning.

The realization of the true meaning of Justice in this reading allows us to further understand the knight of Wands. The activity has become aimless — moving from one thing to another without real results — because it has lost both its base and its purpose. It will stay that way, and the other possibilities will remain blocked, until he can return to his true nature.

The way to that return rests in the image of Justice itself. First, he must recognize the loss. Secondly, he can use the symbol as a means of focusing his mind on the goal. The technique involves a kind of transfer of the self into the image and then a return of the image back into the self so that the qualities become amplified. We will look at this process in more detail in the chapter on meditation. At the time of the reading, we looked primarily at Justice in its aspect of self-examination. What had happened to make him lose his confidence in himself? Did the lack of professional success cause him to turn away from his belief in philosophy and his own place in it? Perhaps he had given so much of himself to the failed relationship that he had surrendered his own way of being, exchanging rationality for emotion, only to find the emotions rejected. During our discussion of these issues he said that he thought he might have made a mistake in coming to Europe, simply because he found it hard to operate without the stimulation and resources of his own culture.

The Queen of Swords (reversed)

The queen of Swords reversed demonstrates how the position of the 'recent past' can derive from the basis. By itself it indicates mental anguish and emotional pain that he has been trying to push away from himself, a reference to the failure of his love affair, and the difficulty of assimilating that experience. Right-side up the queen signifies wisdom gained through sorrow. Upside-down the queen uses her strong mind aggressively, as a defence against anyone she considers her enemy. That category may include herself, for in becoming depressed, or overly critical, or picturing herself as a helpless victim, the queen avoids a genuine examination of her problems.

The theme of examination, and especially the symbol of the sword, returns us to Justice. Again, the upright sword signifies purity of thought and purpose. The single bird flying overhead similarly indicates that the queen seeks only the truth (the card of the king shows two birds, and his sword tilts because of his responsibility to act on his knowledge). Her throne rests on high ground, above the clouds of confusion, and she opens her hand to receive whatever life will bring to her. By looking at what has happened — in the manner of Justice — she allows herself to accept the past, and through acceptance she purifies herself to rise above pain to the level of wisdom. However, like Justice, she appears here reversed.

With the sword and scales of Justice rejected, how can he hold on to the pain of the queen? This pain comes most directly from the failed love affair. At the time of the reading, the relationship had not officially finished. However, the subject was beginning to recognize that it wouldn't work, and would have to end. Thus the queen appears in the recent past as a sign that the situation is ending, but reversed to indicate his difficulty in facing the break-up.

Justice and the ace of Swords push him to rational examination as a kind of liberation. The queen brings him to a similar place through openness and emotional honesty. Like Justitia, she represents the female principle, despite holding the phallic sword. One way to return to the androgynous balance of thought and feeling remains through the feminine quality of emotional vulnerability. So long as he avoids the anguish of the end of the relationship he cannot get beyond the situation or return to his own self, the steps necessary to renew that self in the image of Judgement. For we must remember throughout this reading that it offers him more than a restoration of former balance.

If he can release himself from the current situation, then Judgement offers the possibility of rising to a new level.

The Three of Pentacles (reversed)

We see this potentiality as well in the position of possible outcome. When right-side up, the three of Pentacles indicates mastery and success in the person's chosen field. As the element of Earth Pentacles signify practical matters. Therefore, in its fulfilled upright position, the card signifies professional accomplishments, a master as compared to an apprentice.

Reversed indicates the frustration of that fulfilment, mediocre work, lack of professional development. As the 'possible' it means that under current conditions, he is likely to continue his unsatisfactory pattern of fits and starts in professional work. Nevertheless, even reversed the symbol contains with it the potential for success. He *can* succeed, but it will mean turning around the current direction. In order to work with this card, as well as with the other reversed cards, the subject must take a dual attitude. On the one hand he needs to look honestly at the failures or lacks indicated in the reversed position, while not forgetting the hope embodied in the card itself. On the other hand, he must work towards enacting that hope without forgetting that at present the card has come out reversed. In short, he must keep both sides of the symbol in mind, attempting to compensate whenever he goes too much in one direction or the other.

The medieval concept of a master entailed more than technical accomplishment. Ideally, the master achieved a spiritual development as well, so that awareness of God would infuse his work. The union of spiritual and practical supposedly functioned in all production, no matter how secular the craft might appear on the surface. Its most obvious realization came in the cathedrals and churches. In the three of Pentacles, therefore, we see an artisan at work in a church, shaping an interior wall. Behind him, giving advice, stand a monk and someone who holds the plans of the building. By this symbolism we see that the spiritual and the practical both must inform any true work. If, as the subject believed, philosophy brings spirit into the world, then it can do so only if it achieves a high level of technical ability in such matters as logic, historical knowledge, and so on.

This technical necessity arises from something deeper than the problem of conveying the subject's ideas in an adequate way. An increase in skill means an increase in ideas as well. Compare the philosopher to an artist. Many people assume that a painter learns his craft so that he may execute concepts already formed in his head. In fact, the concepts develop through the work itself. The great mystery of art — or philosophy, or mathematics, or any serious endeavour performed with dedication, love, skill — is the way it discovers truth through the act of trying to portray it. As the subject believed, philosophy does not only carry spirit, it creates it. From the shapeless reservoir of the unconscious, the mind moulds concepts and understanding. The three of Pentacles reminds us that creation of spirit demands technique.

As we leave the possible outcome we must recognize the direct line to it from the basis. Both cards represent a spiritual balance. Justice shows balance in its pure form, the three of Pentacles demonstrates how we carry the balance further by embodying it in reality. And both represent the subject himself, the trump as his archetype, the Minor card as the fulfillment of that archetype. And both are reversed. In the centre, the knight of Wands links the two, giving us yet another view of that card. As well as avoiding current problems, the knight signifies the scattered quality of the subject's previous work. Moving from one thing to another he has not rooted himself in any of the professions he has tried. The 'probable' missed development of the three of Pentacles reversed derives from the knight of Wands as much as from any other influence.

Though Judgement offers an alternative to his current situation it does not directly affect this connection of Justice reversed — knight of Wands — three of Pentacles reversed. These cards form a vertical axis while Judgement lies horizontally across them; in other words he has pushed Judgement away from the movement of his life.

The Eight of Wands (reversed)
Like the knight, the eight of Wands applies a particular image to several questions. When right-side up the card symbolizes things coming to a satisfactory end, movement towards a goal. Upside-down it represents frustration and a continuing movement without any clear destination. As mentioned above it implies that the Wands' energy of the knight, often so creative in other contexts, simply dissipates here. In literal terms, it moves about without going anywhere. This may apply to work, changes of address, projects and plans. In the near future they will not produce satisfactory results.

The eight of Wands sometimes bears the meaning 'arrows of love'. From this we get the reversed meaning of 'arrows of jealousy', which we can extend to the general idea of lovers' quarrels, anger, and so on. The card tells him that as the relationship deteriorates further, the coming weeks will continue in the same hostile mood as the queen of Swords reversed. Just as that card emphasized the internal reaction of suspicion and simmering rage, so the eight of Wands reversed describes the atmosphere between them.

The same mood carries over into the card in the position of self, the ace of Swords reversed. This card, too, carries a specific meaning dealing with troubled relationships — violent emotions, uncontrollable passions, usually directed more toward anger than love. If the queen stood for his side of feeling wounded, a victim, then the Ace shows the desire to strike back. As a weapon, the sword signifies aggression, but upside-down it implies that the weapon controls him rather than the other way around. 'Control' means that his anger overwhelms him. But the image suggests something else. As much as he might try he cannot really direct his violent feelings at the target. He cannot hold on to the sword. We see this as well in the eight of Wands reversed, where the 'arrows' do not hit the ground, but instead fall aimlessly. The female imagery of the queen and the Star suggest a gentle quality in the subject, which makes it hard for him to strike out against an enemy. This situation gives us a simpler view of Justice reversed — that his lover has dealt with him unjustly.

The Ace of Swords (reversed)
The ace of Swords signifies more than violent emotions. As the root card of the suit it stands for the pure qualities of Swords: anger and conflict, but also reason, mind, the discriminative faculty, the ability to think things through, to seek solutions and freedom through the understanding of causes. The ace bears the upright sword of Justice. In the position of self, and in conjunction with Justice as a personal expression, the ace tells him that this approach is necessary for him. It belongs to him. Reversed, however, it says that he has lost control and must somehow seize hold of it again. He needs to focus his mind, to see things clearly and honestly.

The sword on the card pierces through a crown. According to Waite, the deck's designer, the crown symbolizes the material world. The sword, that is the intellect, penetrates through the illusion of immediate reality to the underlying spiritual truth that gives it life. In the act of piercing through something a sword also opens a hole, allowing that which exists on the other side to enter through the gap. In other words, by penetrating material reality to the world of spirit behind it, intellect also allows spirit to emerge into that reality in the form of the thoughts and writing produced by intellect — which returns us again to the subject's view of philosophy. The appearance of the ace of Swords as the card of self, even reversed, implies very strongly that he does indeed belong to philosophy and philosophy to him. Only, he must learn to control and direct his native abilities.

The mountains on the card symbolize the 'abstract truths' (Waite's term) understood through the efforts of a mind tuned to spiritual principles and trained in their application. The same symbol appears on the card of Judgement. The same image on the two cards allows us to consider why he has lost control of the ace. Partly, anger and painful emotions have made it difficult to think clearly. Remember that the ace symbolizes the male principle thrown awry by the 'feminine' experience of wild thoughts and emotions aroused by hurt and anger. The connection to Judgement suggests that fear has also distorted his ability to think clearly and honestly. Subconsciously he rejects Judgement because, as we saw above, the resurrection requires first a serious appraisal of his past experience. Therefore, he will give up the 'mountains' even as he longs for them and believes that he strives to reach them. If someone recognizes philosophy as a personal quest, then the way to it must pass through personal exploration. He has not lost his grip on the ace; he has let go of it because of where it would lead.

If the 'feminine' hot emotions can disrupt the male principle of detached analysis, does that set the two at war with each other? The androgynous symbol of Justice would argue otherwise, but perhaps we must acknowledge that just as these principles act in all human beings, men and women both, so there are times in each person's life when one way of dealing must take precedence. Or maybe the way to one lies through the other. The queen also holds a sword, and when we considered that card we looked at the idea that he can restore his clarity of mind through an acceptance of pain. The outcome, if right-side up, would show the feminine principle embodied in the ease and grace of the Star. Each principle, when seen by itself, remains partial. By using both of them he can respond to Judgement and finally achieve the synthesis implied in the three of Pentacles.

The Nine of Cups (reversed)

The following card, the nine of Cups reversed in the position of environment, demonstrates how a reversed meaning can sometimes show a positive step rather than a loss. If a right-side up card symbolizes something limited, then the reversed can indicate reaching beyond the limitations. In its normal form the nine of Cups stands for relaxation and pleasure: partying, good food, entertainment. Reversed it represents 'truth' and 'liberation', to use Waite's terms. Clearly the reversed meaning does not contradict the upright but rejects it as too narrow for what's needed. In the position of the environment it implies that the failure of the good times in his relationship has spurred him to free himself, but also to seek something deeper in his life. However, because these qualities come from an upside-down card, they lack the positive determination needed to overcome the barrier shown in the rest of the reading. The failure in his environment pushes him to look for something more, but he needs to find that push from within himself.

Temperance (reversed)

Temperance reversed occupies the position of 'hopes and fears'. The card very much encompasses something both longed for and rejected. It shows his fear that he will not gain control over his life, that his emotions will continue to dominate him with violent shifts of love and anger, that he will not take positive and practical steps (for Temperance means action as well as moderation). Now, it might seem that a person would certainly fear such a condition but hardly hope for it. To understand this paradox we need to look at the card's symbolism to see just what it demands of us to achieve its balanced state.

First of all, as discussed in the three card reading above, Temperance insists on calm and a careful blending of opposites. Therefore it would require giving up the powerful emotions of the reversed ace. As unpleasant as these emotions might be, many people find them attractive, almost addictive. They give an intensity to life, which might seem dull at the prospect of doing without them. Also, the concept of moderation might also seem to deny the intense charge the subject sought and sometimes found in philosophy. Just as many academics may treat their subject too much as a lifeless area of professional expertise, so someone dedicated to the spirit of philosophy might come to depend too much on the excitement generated in the search. When that happens we begin first to lose objectivity, and then the very purpose of the activity. Instead of seeking truth we seek stimulation. Temperance cautions against such an attitude, and for this reason Temperance reversed may become desirable.

In order to achieve the calm of Temperance the subject must first overcome his anger. And that may involve simply giving it up. If the only practical step he can take is getting out then what happens to his rage? Temperance proposes letting go of it. Yet many people in such a situation hold on tightly to anger, even cherish it, for it holds out the fantasy of revenge. More, it prevents them from turning their emotions on themselves, once again picturing themselves as victims. Temperance shows a way out of this cycle, by developing a calm and deliberate approach. It represents truly going beyond the past, not trying to escape it, as in the knight of Wands. To the extent that he sees himself as weak and floundering, the subject will long for the autonomy of Temperance and fear its lack. But to the extent that achieving that autonomy requires putting the relationship truly behind him, giving up anger as well as pain, to that extent he rejects Temperance and hopes that it remains something longed for but unrealized.

The Star (reversed)

The final card, the outcome, shows the practical result of hanging on to the situation. The anger becomes turned against itself, and instead of revenge or triumph he ends up depressed, weak. When right-side up the Star depicts openness, an experience of life as joyful and filled with hope. Unlike most of the trump figures the woman is shown naked and completely at ease rather than posed in some formal position, such as the Magician or the High Priestess. She does not struggle or draw on power to accomplish some special task. She is at ease with her own being. In the sequence of trumps the card comes after the Tower, an emblem of destruction, and so the Star shows the calm that follows an outpouring of repressed and even violent emotion. Reversed, as we see it here, this release does not occur and the tension stays locked inside.

The Star represents a higher level of Temperance. In both cards the figure has one foot in water, one on land. The pool symbolizes the unconscious and the person's connection to instinct. The land symbolizes manifestation, indicating that she creates something in the real world. Also in both cards the figure holds two vessels and pours water from them. In Temperance we see an angel, that is, an ideal, adorned with emblems of holiness (God's four letter name, the triangle in the square, and so on). The Star shows simply a woman in her own body. The ideal has become realized. Where the angel pours the water carefully from one cup to another the woman simply pours it out. She no longer needs moderation or caution. Completely open, she knows that she will not lose her balance or sense of herself. To people who see Temperance as too restrictive, or too flat, the Star may appear as a preferred alternative. But in fact, the way to the Star often lies through Temperance. They are not opposites.

The theme of manifestation links the Star to the three of Pentacles, symbol of work and accomplishment. As mentioned above, the possible outcome very often shows a further development beyond the outcome. He cannot achieve his desire — and potential — for professional and spiritual accomplishment until he dissolves the barriers within himself. As we have already seen, the way to the practical synthesis of the three of Pentacles leads through the descent and resurrection of Judgement. In the Star we see the water in the pool stirred up by the emotions poured into it. The Star expresses powerful feelings without letting them overwhelm the mind as in the reversed ace of Swords. In Judgement we see the figures rising out of the water. In both trumps the water symbolizes the unconscious. In the Star (turned right-side up) he no longer fears the hidden material in himself, and in Judgement (turned right-side up) he rises from his own dead past to begin the steps in his new life. But the beginning remains with Justice, the card of the basis, with its sword of truth.

Conclusion

One final question remains about this reading. Is it positive? Should it — did it — leave the subject feeling good about the direction of his life? At the time it produced both weariness and stimulation. As much as he could recognize the issues raised and the great possibilities the reading offered, he still found it daunting to see the kind of assessment he needed to make of his life, his relationship, and himself. For myself, as the reader, I found it very positive. Despite the reversed state of most of the cards, they showed again and again the potential of a whole new beginning, one that could carry through into the realization of the three of Pentacles. But of course, as the reader I did not have to live through it.

CELTIC CROSS TWO

In the following reading we again find Judgement as an image of personal rebirth. But as the context changes, so does the symbol. Seeing the two readings together can help us form a wider understanding of Judgement. They also demonstrate the way a symbol adapts itself to specific situations.

The reading was done for a man who suddenly found himself confronted with his past. In the late '60s he had led a student rebellion at a university, one of the very first actions of that sort in his area. For a time he was well-known, at the centre of a great deal of attention. Then, as so often happens with such movements, the pressure from the outside caused the group to fall apart, and he found himself alone, without the support promised by the other leaders and the people who had joined him. Afterwards, he went on for a while in radical groups, then left them and concentrated on his private life, eventually finding a satisfying career. Fifteen years later a magazine decided to do an article about the strike, and called him for an interview. To his great surprise he found that the request triggered a panic in him. All the bad feeling, all the troubled emotions of that time came back, and he discovered he had never settled his feelings about the event, but only submerged them, assuming he was rid of them because of the time that had passed. Unsure what to do about the article he asked me for a Tarot reading, and when we laid out the cards they addressed the question of why he should feel so strongly about an event so long ago.

We chose the king of Swords as significator. When he'd mixed them they came out as follows.

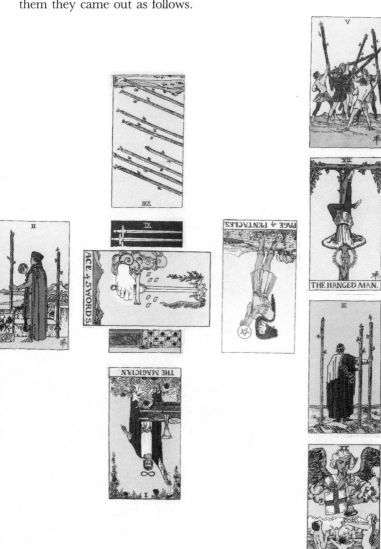

Aside from the page of Pentacles and the three trump cards, the reading contains all Swords and Wands. As the active and to some extent aggressive cards, they stress the conflict in himself and his memories of battling with others. The absence of Cups indicates his inability to summon any benign emotions about his subject, despite his hope, shown in the Hanged Man, to free himself from other people's opinions or reactions. But even though Swords and Wands both show battle scenes they signify very different approaches. The change from the first to the second indicates that he can transform the situation by drawing on his accomplishments, and the life he's made for himself in the intervening years.

The Nine of Swords

The first card, the nine of Swords, depicts the pain aroused and the seriousness of the problem. It clears up any doubts that he might be exaggerating his reactions. Sometimes we can understand a card better if we compare it to another, similar (or opposite) card that might have shown up in the same situation. In this case, the ten of Swords, a picture of a man lying on the ground with ten swords in his back, would also have symbolized the subject's troubled feelings, but would have implied that he was overstating the situation.

For the ten carries the meaning of hysteria and excess. The nine, however, signifies genuine sorrow, it tells him that he has not become carried away, but is addressing a real problem. In the picture a woman sits up in bed, weeping with nine swords hanging above her. The nightclothes imply that her anguish has woken her up in the middle of the night. When we remember that the call for an interview catapulted the subject into something he thought totally behind him, we can understand the aptness of the image. The interview has woken him from a long sleep. The swords hanging behind and above the woman symbolize the way in which his unresolved past has always threatened him, even when he thought he no longer cared about it.

The night-time aspect of the nine contrasts very strongly with the sunshine/day symbolism of the Wands cards. The nine evokes the way he has buried the problem, ignoring it for years. Now the past has emerged to eclipse the bright quality of his current life. Judgement, in the position of self, indicates that he must descend into the night in order to rise out of it.

The Ace of Swords

The second card (one of the three this reading shares with the previous one) shows him literally grabbing hold of his emotions. If the nine indicates genuine pain rather than hysteria, then the ace tells him not to overstate his reaction. He mustn't indulge himself in guilt or self-pity. A rigorous card, the ace of Swords demands a firm grip on the emotions. In some contexts, when the emotions need to come out, such a grip might arise from or lead to repression. It works here because the other cards, especially Judgement and the five of Wands, indicate that the sorrow does indeed belong to the past and he can, in fact, release himself from it. This does not contradict the nine, it just tells him he can do something about it.

Nor does the ace advise him to ignore the situation. The idea of analysis, so important to the previous subject, applies here as well, for it tells him he can think the situation through and in that way gain some control over it. Again, if this sounds like over obvious advice, we should consider the various cards that might have counselled acceptance, or countering pain with pleasure and friendship. To give yet another possibility, the eight of Cups would have told him to put it behind him. Instead, the reading advises him to ponder the past and his own reactions to it. He must think hard about what has happened. By doing so he will move from night into day. And it tells him he can do this. He does not have to accept the pain he feels. Instead of letting the swords hang over him he can take them in hand.

The drops of light falling on either side of the sword form the Hebrew letter yod, first letter of God's four letter name. They symbolize grace, and together with the image of a hand coming out of a cloud, represent the idea of a gift. All the aces come to us this way, as something 'given' to us by life at that moment. Usually the gift of an ace refers to a general experience of the suit's qualities.

Here, however, we can see the idea of the gift very specifically in the form of the magazine article. If the editor had not requested the interview the subject would not have experienced the sudden anguish of memory. He also would have missed the chance to identify vague dissatisfactions (shown in the following two cards) and then to do something about them. Living in the light, he would have allowed a certain part of him to remain hidden in the dark.

The Magician (reversed)

The Magician reversed in the position of basis builds on this same imagery. First of all, the card signifies the creative solar principle, and thus the idea of light. Upside-down, that light does not shine with its full force. We will look at what that means in a moment, but first we must consider the other images relating it to the first two cards. The Magician grasps his wand firmly as he raises it toward heaven. By thus taking hold of his power he connects it to the source of his strength in life, drawing it into himself for the purpose of manifesting it in the real world (symbolized by the finger pointing down at the flowers). But again, a reversed card means he cannot hold on properly to the power, and so, instead of directing it outward, he allows it to control him.

What does 'power' mean here? In general, the term applies to the ability he has shown to make something of his life. Coming from a situation in which his whole way of being had fallen to pieces (for his radical activities after university had brought him to a dead end) he had built a new life for himself. And yet, a part of him still felt scattered, unable to find satisfaction or feel truly in control of his life. For power also means the force of his anger.

Subjectively the Magician reversed feels like weakness, passivity when action is needed, confusion. But the energy is there; he does not know how to direct it. Afraid of actually wielding his anger as power, he backs away from it, and so it controls him, instead of the other way around. As the basis it says he had taken this approach all along, avoiding the pain by not thinking about it. The Magician's wand symbolizes the creative power in a person's life. The transformation from the wand into the sword of the ace means that at this time he can seize hold of the energy by first of all putting his reactions in perspective, and then analysing the emotions brought up from the past. In so doing he changes the power back into the creative force, Wands. No Swords cards appear after the centre and the crossing.

The gnostics (a varied group of early Christians who greatly

influenced esoteric thought in Europe) preached that the body traps
a portion of God's light in matter. It becomes the task of the soul
to free itself through 'gnosis', that is, knowledge of truth. In the reading
we see a mundane enactment of this sacred drama. The Magician
reversed represents the trapped light. Indeed, in its symbolism, the
Magician signifies the light, or power of God, passing through the
body as an open channel. Reversed, the light gets trapped. In terms
of the subject's life he has used the activities and success of the past
years as a barrier or a coating to keep the light away from
consciousness, for he had come to associate it with pain. We will see
this image as well in the wall surrounding the two of Wands. The
ace of Swords represents gnosis — at it does philosophically, when
we remember that the crown symbolizes matter and the sword pierces
through it. By cutting through both the intervening years and his
own complicated reactions he liberates the trapped portion of himself.

The Magician reversed appears in the basis, at the root of his life.
A certain part of him has always remained trapped in that moment
in the past. Because he didn't resolve the conflicts at the time, he
never became free of them. Judgement as the card of self indicates
that the time has finally come to go through that delayed release.

The Two of Wands
The two of Wands in the recent past also carries the idea of something
trapped or closed in, but in a more muted way. The card represents
success and an established life, but also a feeling that life has bound
him in and separated him from the direct world of experience. Thus
we see the man standing inside the stone wall of his castle, looking
out at nature. The castle belongs to him but he also belongs to it.
Wands' energy often encounters this problem. It involves itself in
projects and ambitions and then, when it accomplishes them it finds
itself bound in by practical responsibilities. Notice that the figure in
the card looks outward. He does not know how to look within himself,
and within his life for satisfaction or peace. Waite compares him to
Alexander, who conquered the world and then cried because success
left him with nothing further to do. He could only exist, could only
maintain his balance by continually directing himself outward, at the
world. The figure in the picture requires Wands, sunshine and a
constant look forward, to the future, to keep his excitement. Security
chafes at him, it confines. And at the same time, he knows that
somewhere something is wrong. He does not want to look at the past,
does not want to think about it. When it finally arises, as shown in
the nine of Swords, the night sweeps over him. He does not know,

does not trust himself to know, that he can make peace with the past. And by doing so, in Judgement, he will free the energy, returning him to enthusiasm and action, as shown in the five of Wands, the outcome card.

Many people beginning to work with Tarot cards and the Celtic cross assume that 'recent past' must refer to some single event close to the present. But when 'basis' demonstrates a core situation, then 'recent' can depict a pattern that extends over years. The two of Wands shows what the subject has made of his life since he abandoned his radical involvement. A success, a genuine member of the establishment, he still misses the days when he accepted no restraints, no confinements. He has not learned how to keep that quality of excitement in the life he lives now. More, he has not recognized that the discontent and boredom he feels come at least partly from the piece of himself which has remained in the unresolved past. Now the past has returned to him, forcing him to deal with what he thought he had left behind. The merchant in the two of Wands grips one Wand; he has bolted the other firmly into place. He keeps a tight control on that outward directed energy of the suit. But the inner wand of himself, the wand of the Magician, has remained out of his control. He must grab hold of it as the ace of Swords.

The Eight of Wands (reversed)

From the previous reading we have learned some things about the reversed eight of Wands, the card in the position here of possible outcome. It tells us first of all that the situation might continue without coming to a satisfactory end. The concept of jealousy applies here not to romance but to the possible conflicts and fresh recriminations that might arise because of the article. The subject feared that such battles might break out. While the seriousness of the past conflicts gave a real basis for such fears, they now arose largely from his own difficulty in taking hold of the situation. The eight of Wands reversed derives from the reversed Magician.

And yet, the reading indicates that these things will not, in fact, happen. Here we see an example of how the position of possible outcome illuminates the actual outcome by showing us an alternative reality, one that might have developed, but will not. The possible outcome demonstrates what would result if he simply remained trapped in his anxieties. Instead, the five of Wands shows him liberated from that anxiety. The difference between the two sends us on a search for the causes of this liberation. Partly it results because the article has brought the trouble to the surface. Inside for so long it has hampered him until he could not even recognize the difficulty but only observe a certain dissatisfaction and inability to enjoy what he was doing. Now that he must look at it he can prevent letting it work on him indefinitely (the movement without destination of the reversed eight of Wands). He can discover that the time has come for Judgement.

The Page of Pentacles (reversed)
The page of Pentacles reversed occupies the near future position. As a page, it symbolizes a student, and therefore his return in consciousness to his university days. Upside-down, therefore, it shows that despite the positive outcome, he will remain for a time agitated. Of course, such a 'prediction' follows from the situation. What is important is the temporary quality of the position. In short, the card does not only predict disturbance but says that the disturbance will pass, it will not claim a real part of him. If we compare this card with the nine of Swords we see that the trouble is already beginning to pass, for the page of Pentacles presents a much lighter image, someone distracted rather than someone in anguish.

The specific meanings of the page of Pentacles reversed include bemusement. Something leads a person astray from his proper concerns. The concept derives from the fact that Pentacles represent work and practical matters, so that the page reversed means literally a student departing from his studies. In a position of past experience in this reading the card might have indicated the way in which his politics took him away from his learning. In the place of immediate future, however, (for in this reading 'near' means 'immediate', with no gap, but extending for a period of time) it signifies an over concern with the surface of things — the danger of scandal, embarrassment, the details of the article and its appearance in the magazine. Again the reading can relieve his mind, because it describes these matters as surface and temporary. What should concern him here is why he lets himself wander off into these superficial worries. Judgement tells him, 'Don't bother yourself with these things. They'll pass.' At the same time it also says 'Concern yourself with what really matters. You've let the night rise up over you. Now you must go into it, in order to free the sun.'

In this reading we see a distinct separation between the cross and the staff. The first six cards outline the problem with its history, its development in the present and its possible extensions. The last four show the solutions. Each one contributes a step towards the liberation of energy shown in the final card. When we remember the importance of the stick symbolism in the Magician and the various Wands cards we can view the four cards of the staff as the subject grabbing hold of himself and the problem.

Judgement

As always, and especially in this reading, the root of the staff rests in the self. The previous reading showed us a good deal about the symbolism of Judgement, and much of that symbolism applies here. We have seen as well the graphic connection to the darkness of the nine of Swords, the reversal of the solar principle in the Magician reversed, and the need to liberate that principle in the Wands cards. Above all, Judgement in the position of self tells him simply that the problem belongs to the past. He can rise out of that past so that it no longer affects his present.

We have looked at the reversed Magician as primarily weakness and disturbance. But Judgement reminds us that when darkness overcomes the light it can, in fact, produce benefits. In the nine of Swords we saw the female principle raised up. It emerged in pain and sorrow, but it could only come forth that way. He had buried it for too long. Only by taking on the aspects of Swords could it force its way to the surface, disguised as a victim of suffering imposed from outside. Jungian psychologists use the term 'anima' to refer to a man's feminine side, and 'shadow' to indicate the repressed material of the ego. In the nine of Swords we see a graphic merging of the two. Because he held down the feminine — in this case, the willingness to accept the experience instead of opposing it — because he put himself so much into the outward looking masculine approach of Wands, he in fact achieved neither. The female principle remained submerged to rise up finally as darkness overtaking him, while the male — the Magician — remained distorted and trapped. Judgement, by emphasizing the deliberate and conscious descent into the past experience, in fact liberates both the masculine and feminine approaches to life. We see this in the man and woman rising from their tombs.

But remember that the child — the son — also rises. Something fresh and unified is liberated. Because he has resolved the experiences of his youth he emerges rejuvenated, a child again. In Judgement he becomes his own son, and when we reach the top of the staff, the five of Wands, we will see that the pun of 'son' and 'sun' becomes reality in the image of youthful fire. Judgement in the position of self tells him that he does not belong in the past, he can and will rise out of it.

The Three of Wands

The three of Wands in the environment signifies first of all that the article will not seriously harm him. The card carries no destructive or aggressive qualities. More important, the image shows a goal for his relation to his environment, and to the situation that began with such disturbance. We see the figure on a hilltop looking out at boats sailing beneath him. The golden tint gives the picture a feeling of sunset. We can consider the card as showing a person looking at his past. He stands calmly and considers what has gone before. In the nine of Swords the past rose up at him and he could not bear to face it; the woman in the picture has covered her face with her hands. Here, however, he has passed the crisis, he has found firm ground to stand on, and no longer fears what he will see when he looks at his world.

The image of standing on the hill suggests that he grounds himself by recognizing the reality of the life he has built. Not a barrier against the past, as in the Magician reversed (where, in fact, he separates himself from the ground of being symbolized in the flowers), not an artificial enclosure as in the two, but a real base of accomplishment, so that ultimately the past can no longer hold him hostage. The present has become real enough to free him. At the same time the present must include the past, and the hill on which he stands symbolizes the reality of his life as a whole. Remember that in both the ace of Swords and Judgement the mountains signify abstract truth. Here he stands on a hill of knowledge, enabling him to gaze peacefully at his life. He gazes across the water at mountains similar to those on the ace (both are coloured purple). He keeps an awareness of principles and truth, understood through the experience of Judgement, but he does not try to live in that pure realm. Instead he allows it to inform his understanding. He has chosen to keep himself on this side of the water, in the world of activity and success. In contrast to the Magician reversed and the two of Wands, that world does not conceal or confine the light but draws its strength from it. As in the two he grips one of the wands. There, however, he used the force of his character to close himself in against his environment. Here he uses it to open himself up to the outside. In the two, the extra wand could only stand if bolted firmly to the wall; he needed to control all the energy with conscious purpose. Here, the two wands not held, root themselves in the Earth.

If the three shows him at peace with the past and rooted in the present, it looks to the future as well (like the three of Pentacles in the last reading the card represents a synthesis). If the ships are coming home they represent memories. But if they sail away then they stand for exploration, new projects. The freed Wands' energy once again moves outward, once more seeking adventure, but now with a more secure base in himself. He sends his ships out but remains on firm ground. That is, he no longer identifies totally with his activities, as in the two, when success closed around him. He understands the distinction between himself and what he does in the world. As an interesting footnote to this reading, the subject moved to New York several months later. There he began a new career, as well as getting married and having a child — a son.

The three of Wands signifies a goal for his relationship to his environment. The push to make that goal real comes from the card beneath it, Judgement. Success depends also on the next card, the Hanged Man, in the position of hopes and fears. In a sense, Judgement pushes from below (something experienced within the self) while the Hanged Man pulls from above (his hope for what his life can become). The previous reading demonstrated the ambivalence of hope and fear in a single image. In this reading, my sense of the card in its context — the rest of the reading with its direction of creative release — told me that in this case the desire remained pure, unmixed with the dread.

The Hanged Man
In one meaning the Hanged Man symbolizes independence from other people's opinions. He hangs upside-down partly to signify his separation from the mass of society with its conventions and rigid morality. Disturbed by his own fear of controversy, the subject sought such independence and we can see his hope as just that. But independence cannot just happen. The Hanged Man achieves freedom from pressure through a special relation to life and to himself. He has rooted himself so deeply in the rhythms of life that public opinion, scandal, and any other such vagaries cannot blow him aside. Instead of taking hold of the Wands' creative power and wielding it for some external purpose, he has attached himself to the tree. When we looked at the Magician reversed we saw how the upside-down image indicated the loss of direction. If he cannot properly direct his power then it becomes trapped inside him, resulting in weakness and confusion. But the man on the tree already hangs upside-down, and the light shines about his head. By reversing the usual way of dealing with the world — that is, confronting it and overcoming — the Hanged Man allows life to open up around him. He has found a true base, a true connection.

These values underlie the Hanged Man as a hope. The subject

could not delineate them consciously, and yet they emerge into his
life from his desire for independence and peace within himself. As
a Major Arcana card, the Hanged Man symbolizes principles. The
way in which these principles can emerge into reality shows in the
Minor card below it, the three of Wands. Though that too remains
a goal at this point it embodies what can become of his yearning for
the Hanged Man.

The Five of Wands

As mentioned above, the five of Wands outcome shows a rejuvenation
and a release of energy. It depicts the Wands, energy being wielded
forcefully, but without anger. In practical terms it says that the article
will bring some conflict, but the subject will not find it fearful or
disturbing. He has finally left it behind him. The imagery shows youths
battling, and therefore returns him to the past arguments and
recriminations of the university days. But now it represents anger
released by the publication of the article, anger which no longer binds
him. Because of Judgement and the Hanged Man he can let his rage
out and discover that he had gone beyond it. All those years ago,
at the time of the strike, he found it impossible to accept his own
aggression towards the others. Thus, the Magician became turned
upside-down, distorted into the external activities of the two of Wands.
Here, in the five, he allows aggression to surface and finds that it
frees rather than cripples. These meanings apply specifically to the
article. In a wider sense, the card shows that life and the struggle
to succeed have once more become exhilarating.

Earlier in the reading we looked at alternatives that might have
appeared, but didn't. Here too we can compare the five of Wands
to another card, the five of Swords.

The Swords card would have signalled defeat, a sense of shame and weakness. It would have carried the initial reaction — the nine of Swords — to a bitter conclusion. It was partly the fear of such weakness that kept the subject from releasing his anger for so many years. But instead of staying with Swords, the reading moved into Wands, a move that derives from Judgement in the position of self, allowing him to take hold of the ace of Swords. He overcomes the illusion of helplessness. The reading begins in anguish. It ends in excitement.

CELTIC CROSS THREE

The previous readings showed the sort of information the Tarot can give to a person. They described the way in which a situation has developed and the way it will go. More important, they set the person within the situation and within him or herself. They placed the subject at the centre, showing past and future, self and others, and the ways in which things reverberate from that centre. They set the person and the person's problems in a wider context — his or her history, influences, archetypal symbols and through the symbols, psychic and cultural history.

And yet, as much as these readings tell us, they leave us with the subject of how to continue. To some extent, the reading will tell the subject what approach to take — analysis, or acceptance, or action, and so on. But he or she must find a way to this approach alone. But a symbol can do more than give advice. Properly used, a Tarot reading can help the person to transform or develop the situation itself. In discussing Justice as a personal archetype in the first Celtic cross reading I hinted at one method of using the symbol to overcome the barrier to the kinds of experience the symbol represents.

In the following reading the subject followed these procedures in practice. The results, as we will see, are not some dramatic reversal of her whole life. The reading, and the work she does with it, do not even ensure a particular development. In fact, at the time of this writing, the situation had not resolved itself in one direction or another. What the symbols helped her do was move towards overcoming the limitations shown in the reading.

The subject was a woman who had worked with the Tarot herself and who had come to me before for readings (as with several other people whose readings appear in this book). The reading dealt with a romantic triangle, a situation that probably prompts more people to consult the Tarot than any other problem. Usually the person wants to know how the triangle will resolve itself. 'Will my husband forget his girl friend and stay with me?' 'Will my friend leave her lover and come with me?' 'Which one should I choose?' Each of these questions have spurred people to come for readings. In each one, the subject assumes that someone will drop out and a couple will continue. The subject of this reading, however, came with a different attitude. Neither she, nor the others involved, wanted the situation to break apart. On the contrary, they all sought — at least consciously — for the situation to continue, but harmoniously.

The subject had lived with her lover, another woman, for several years in what they termed a 'committed relationship'. That is, they intended to stay together, and to work hard to overcome any problems that might arise between them. Despite this commitment, however, they had agreed, some time before the period of the reading, that they would not be strictly monogamous. They would occasionally have other lovers. These relationships did not arise very often and were never kept secret. Nor did they usually last more than a few months.

Now, however, something different had occurred. The subject's friend had become involved with someone new, and after several months these two had come to realize they could not think of their relationship as temporary or casual. The subject's friend had not changed her feelings for the subject. The subject herself did not fear that her lover would leave and go with the new person. Nevertheless, for the first time she felt threatened, fearful for the future. We should note that the subject did not consider the third woman as an enemy, or condemn her for 'interfering' in her relationship. She and this woman were friends from before the situation and continued to be friends, though as we shall see from the reading, this connection had become strained, perhaps more so than the subject wanted to acknowledge.

Many people, looking on this subject from the outside, would say to the subject 'You've got to put your foot down.' Or they would advise the subject's partner, 'If you love her you'll stop hurting her.' In looking at this reading we must remember that the subject herself hoped that the three of them could work the situation out in some way beneficial to all of them.

The reading came a day after the subject and her lover had talked for a long time about what had happened, where they were going, and what they might do to make it go more smoothly. She came to the reading with no specific questions, but only a desire for guidance. She came, in fact, seeking symbols to help her go forward.

For the significator we used the queen of Wands, the card she'd used for herself for several years. Interestingly, she had used, before the queen of Wands, the knight of Cups, and at times she had described the queen of Cups as a 'goal' for herself. Both these cards appeared in the reading, the knight as the outcome, the queen — reversed — as the possible outcome. The knight of Swords, which the subject's partner used as her significator in her own readings, also appears in the reading, in the position of basis.

When the subject had mixed the cards we turned them up as follows:

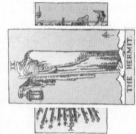

The first card that struck me was the three of Cups reversed, not so much for its significance as for its (expected) appearance. In recent years various people have attempted a similar broadening of the traditional couple relationship. As a Tarot reader, I have seen a number of people seeking advice about the sort of situation shown here. Time after time in these readings the three of Cups has symbolized the hope of harmony. Because the picture shows three women joyously dancing together it embodies perfectly the ideal of a three way relationship (the symbolism does not apply only to lesbian relationships, and certainly not only to romantic situations, but to any three people supporting and encouraging each other). At times, when I've done a series of readings for someone going through such an experience, the card has shown up, upright, in the beginning in the position of hope or possible outcome. Later, if things didn't work out, the three of Cups would appear reversed, in a position such as the recent past. Its upside-down appearance here did not necessarily signal failure. Instead, it pointed out the current difficulties the subject faced, and helped her to recognize a certain hostility in herself towards the others.

As the subject later told me, the other two people had also laid the cards that same day. In that reading the three of Cups came out, right-side up, in the possible outcome. The variance between the two readings did not indicate a contradiction, but only a difference in outlook. We will look more at that other reading at the end of this one.

I expected the three of Cups to appear and it did. I expected as well that the Lovers might show up, either right-side up or reversed, but it failed to appear. Nor did any of the other cards symbolizing couples (for example: the two and ten of Cups, the four of Wands, the ten and five of Pentacles). This lack did not signal that the subject's relationship would collapse. If a breakup had loomed ahead, then the Lovers or similar cards would have appeared, only reversed. Instead, as we shall see with the Hermit, the reading turns her attention to herself. She must look within herself for strength, understanding, development. We see in this reading trumps seven, eight, and nine, the Chariot, Strength, and the Hermit. Number six, the Lovers, speaks to us by its absence. (An interesting point, $7 + 8 + 9 = 24$, which reduces to 6, the number of the Lovers. Can we say from this that the achievement of the cards of self-creation will return her to the card of union?)

The Ten of Wands (reversed)
The first card was the ten of Wands reversed. Its presence in the centre signified that the reading concerned the subject's ability to handle

the situation, but also her desire to continue it. For the card symbolizes responsibility, and therefore reversed it may indicate a desire to throw down that responsibility, to say, 'I want nothing more to do with this.' As the one who 'stays at home' as she put it, she had come to feel she was taking part in this experiment solely for the benefit of the other people. Rationally she did not really believe this. When we look at the knight of Swords we will see that she herself had pushed for an open relationship. More important, she considered that success of the experiment would benefit her as well, and not simply because she too could look forward to outside affairs. In discussing her attitude, she told me that she believed that this situation could strengthen her primary relationship by allowing her lover and herself to become more independent without (she hoped) weakening the powerful bond between them. The emotions, however, often operate on an atavistic level. They look at trouble in the same way young children often look at problems. 'Why are they doing this to me? It's unfair. Take it away.' Therefore, the ten of Wands suggests the feeling of having accepted a burden from other people, of taking the problem on her shoulders. Reversed, it shows her throwing the burden down.

Nor is this denial necessarily unproductive. Many people have a tendency to try to act in a nice way, so that other people will admire them. When I asked the subject about this she told me that she sometimes felt she acted from a desire to do the right thing, rather than from what she really wanted. In this situation, too, she had gone along with her lover's wishes partly because she had committed herself, and wanted to follow that commitment. But there was also a part of her that just wanted to appear admirable and 'nice'. Thus the ten of Wands reversed may have signalled petulance, but it also indicated a realization that she could not continue to act 'correctly' when it went against her own feelings. In short, she needed to break away from the situation or else find a more solid base for continuing.

Like the three of Cups in the special case of triangles, the ten of Wands appears often in relationship readings in general. One client of mine received it in virtually every reading she did during a period of conflict between her and her boyfriend. She began to joke about putting an ad in the paper: 'Woman will carry ten sticks to small village'. For her it meant a tendency to keep any complaints or anger within herself, as if she mustn't trouble him. Finally resentment would overcome her sense of obligation. Then she would throw down the sticks and confront him, but by then everything would have become inflated. Further, she often found that after the blow-up she would return to her pattern of holding in her anger. Once again, the ten of Wands would right itself. In discussing this problem once, she told me that she visualized it as throwing the sticks behind or in front of her. If behind, then she truly wanted to rid herself of her exaggerated sense of responsibility. If in front, then she was throwing a fit, but in fact would soon pick up the sticks again and continue on to the village — a goal she never reached.

For this subject as well the question became where she was throwing the sticks. If behind she would seek changes for her own benefit rather than from a desire to appear nice. If before, she was giving way to that resentment that builds up whenever people act from duty rather than desire.

These ways of looking at the card focus on the specific symbolism of burdens. But the card also relates to the other Wands cards in the reading: the queen as significator, the Ace, the Hermit with his stick, and the wand of power held by the Charioteer. In that sense, the ten wands signify her strength and ability to function in life. Instead of using this power creatively or as an expression of joy, she had expended her own strength for external purposes. She was not living for herself.

This sacrifice arose partly from that desire to appear nice, but also from a fear of her own emotions, especially jealousy and anger, qualities she did not wish to recognize in herself or express to other people. The ten reversed could signify that she would no longer cover herself with a false sense of duty — or it could mean she had let her strength become so scattered, so directed outward, that she had become splintered. The ace of Wands in the near future shows a return to unity, and a sense of a new beginning. (This visual interpretation of the 'splintered' wands and their restoration in the ace comes originally from a client in another reading. See page 118, Work Cycle Two.) The issue becomes partly whether she can carry this return forward. Strength reversed in the position of hopes and fears shows her doubts about her own resources.

Doing a reading for someone who knows the cards can pose certain problems. True, the person's understanding of the symbolism can help her or him to work on the reading. At the same time, a knowledge of the cards' textbook meanings can lead the subject to jump to conclusions about a card's function. Usually these are negative conclusions, for one thing we learn from doing Tarot readings is the surprising pessimism of most people. The average subject will go into a reading hoping for the best, but expecting the worst. And if they know that, say, the Tower means destruction then the sight of that card will lead them to ignore all others and assume everything already lies in ruins. I do not mean to suggest that a reader should ignore or avoid the subject's reactions. On the other hand, pessimism usually comes from fear rather than a real response to the symbol.

The Hermit

In this reading the sight of the Hermit as the crossing card roused the subject's fear that her lover would leave her. She would end up alone, a 'hermit'. Actually, from her knowledge of the cards she should have realized that the trump does not mean loneliness. As we have seen, an end to the relationship would have appeared more directly. In fact, the reading does not tell her that her lover *won't* leave her. It simply throws the development of the situation back on herself. This refusal to predict is in many ways the essential quality of this reading, and a recognition of that quality is the first step to understanding what the reading tells her.

The Hermit represents a positive development out of the ten of Wands reversed. That card showed her perceptions of acting for others, according to a code of niceness. Reversed, the card indicated her desire not to continue. The Hermit shows her beginning to rely on her own needs and understanding. As the second card of the middle line of seven trumps, the Hermit traditionally symbolizes a turn away from outer demands to pursue a path of knowledge and awareness. In the centre card she threw down the ten scattered wands of external pressure. In the Hermit she takes up the staff of self. The card signifies the need to understand herself, and to use her own feelings as the basis for her actions.

On its most direct level the Hermit reminds her of her original belief that the situation would provide 'benefits' for her. One of these benefits, as she told me when we discussed the card, was the idea of time for herself. When she did not allow insecurity to threaten her she had enjoyed the moments alone, the sense of independence and of sometimes doing things on her own rather than always as part of a couple. The Hermit helped remind her of this attitude which had become lost in anxiety and jealousy.

In its place in the Major Arcana the Hermit symbolizes a retreat from the outward concerns of society for the purpose of looking inwards for truth and the beginnings of transformation. In this reading, she must reject the extreme sense of responsibility shown in the ten of Wands in order to find out what *she* wants, what *she* needs to do. The ten wands symbolized her scattered self. The single staff of the Hermit shows a return to unified purpose by withdrawing her attention from the others and relying on her own perceptions.

If we have linked the Hermit's staff to the suit of Wands, there are also differences. While Wand means creative energy, the trump symbolizes wisdom. The Hermit appears as the archetype of the 'wise old man' who has stepped out of society to climb the mountain of truth (remember the mounts on Judgement) and now lights the way for others. Thus, the subject does not turn just to her own activities, but to a path of knowledge. She must seek understanding within herself. In some versions of this card the lantern encloses the star. In his description of this card Waite makes the point that the lantern allows the light to shine openly. He wished to say that the person who seeks esoteric knowledge does not do so selfishly, but rather with a sense of obligation to lead others who will come after. In its more mundane uses in this reading the open lantern suggests that she does not give up her sense of responsibility by throwing down the ten wands and picking up the staff. Rather, she does away with false obligation. By returning to a sense of herself she will find a true responsibility. This idea, that even in seeking herself she cannot escape her concern for the others, is one of the most difficult to accept. We will see, in her meditation with the queen of Cups, that only by loving the others can she find her own strength.

As with the ace of Swords in our previous reading the card calls for the 'masculine' faculty of thought and discernment. However, the ace, like all aces, symbolizes a pure approach. The Hermit carries a more complex meaning. If we divide the Major Arcana into three lines of seven, then the Hermit occupies the same place in the second line as the High Priestess in the line above. Similarly, the female Strength comes below the male Magician. The second line indicates a reversal of values by reversing the sexual polarity. The change does not present a mirror image. The reversal combines qualities of the male and female principles to produce further developments. The High Priestess symbolizes intuition, a sense of the wholeness and mystery of life. The Hermit keeps this instinctive understanding and adds to it knowledge, rational examination that surfaces when we turn from the outer world to dwell within the unconscious of the High Priestess.

The Hermit is number nine in the Major Arcana. By ancient tradition, this number belongs to the mysteries of the lunar goddess, whose crescent emblem appears at the feet of the High Priestess. The card of the Moon is 18, $1 + 8 = 9$, returning us to the Hermit, follower of the lunar path. As we have seen in the previous reading, the Magician stands for the solar principle, the High Priestess for the lunar — that is, the Magician acts, directing energy outward, while the High Priestess reflects and receives, like the moon, drawing energy and awareness inwards. By withdrawing from the outside world the Hermit partakes of the High Priestess's quality of inner direction. But he does not give up the male principle of contemplation. Where the High Priestess's veil conceals the formlessness of the unconscious, the Hermit begins to give shape and clarity to instinctive perceptions. The lantern symbolizes the light of the intellect shining in the darkness of the self. Therefore, the reading stresses that she must return to herself, but must think about the emotions and perceptions that rise to the surface. While the Hermit turns away from the solar world to enter the dark, he does so as an ascent. Traditionally we think of hermits as retreating to caves, symbols of the womb of the goddess, and thus of the perfect unity that precedes consciousness. In the Tarot Hermit we see him standing on the mountain. The goal is not the abandonment of consciousness, but its elevation. She must not 'retreat' into her own feelings, but allow them to rise up so that she can begin to understand her real needs and responsibilities.

Both the High Priestess and the Hermit carry qualities of silence. The High Priestess's veil and closed scroll symbolize the impossibility of describing instinctive mystery. The Hermit's silence comes from his solitude. He leaves society to insure he will not distract himself communicating with others. He can listen to himself. This theme in the reading tells the subject she should try not to talk constantly about the situation with the others, but wait until she knows her own mind, a knowledge that must develop by itself in the silence and solitude of the Hermit. Eventually she must communicate with the other two. First, however, she must communicate with herself.

Nevertheless, the Hermit's silence is not that of his mistress, the High Priestess. There, she maintains her sense of wholeness by not attempting to speak. But the Hermit will speak of what he has learned. Holding his lamp, he wishes to light the way. The period of silence allows him to formulate his thoughts. A period of withdrawal will allow the subject to return emotionally to the others with something more worthwhile than agitation or resentment. The Hermit carries a great sense of return. Return to wholeness, return to the self, return to peace, to belief. And finally, return to others. The image serves as a powerful counter to the ten scattered wands beneath it.

Both the High Priestess and the Hermit convey a feeling of darkness: the hidden temple of the second trump, the night solitude of the ninth. Our cultural history pushes us to equate darkness with evil, ignorance, fear. But darkness also carries creative potential. Just as the foetus grows in the dark womb, so works of art must develop in the hidden side of the self. A painter or writer who knows ahead of time everything she or he wishes to convey will produce a perfectly crafted — and perfectly dead — piece of work. Self knowledge too emerges from darkness. We do not know ahead of time who we are. We must discover it. We must create it, a merging of the Magician and the High Priestess. A hermit, or a shaman, or an ascetic, retreats to a dark cave or the wilderness (away from the light of civilization) in order to return to the greater darkness of the unconscious. The subject must not fear solitude or her own sense of darkness within herself, but use them as a way of returning to her own feeling for life. The meditation at the end will show how the Hermit's darkness becomes a source of strength.

The reading ends with the knight of Cups. This card describes a kind of lesser version of the Hermit, still withdrawn, but more troubled by the outside. The true fulfilment of the Hermit, her return to the world, would be in the queen of Cups, but that card comes out reversed. The failure to carry the Hermit forward derives from the Chariot and Strength upside-down in the positions of self and hopes and fears. These two cards, numbered seven and eight, represent values and qualities necessary to support the Hermit, nine, in its attempt to go beyond the ten of Wands reversed. Lacking in will (the Chariot), not believing in her own Strength, she allows her sense of purpose to drift and becomes passive in her solitude (the knight of Cups) while in fact losing the Hermit's self-sufficiency. The task of the reading becomes the transformation of the Chariot, Strength, and the queen of Cups. The 'mandala' given at the end of the reading was constructed to help the subject work towards this goal.

The Knight of Swords

The knight of Swords occupied the position of basis. As mentioned above, the subject's lover used the knight of Swords as significator in her own readings. Therefore, we can interpret that card to imply that the subject had given herself over to the other person's influence. She had allowed someone else's personality, someone else's desires and ideas, to become the basis of *her* current situation. No wonder the Hermit called her to return to herself. And no wonder the reversed ten of Wands indicated she had gone too far with her desire to be nice and to do the right thing. To say that she let someone else become her basis means just that. She *let* this happen. Despite the forceful quality of the knight, the subject herself had chosen this path, she herself took up the ten wands (and threw them down again) and now she alone must find her own path up the mountain of the Hermit.

The reading contains no signs of oppression by others (such as the eight of Swords) or the need to battle against anyone's influence. Instead, it sends her back to herself.

The knight of Swords may signify an actual person, but it also represents certain characteristics. Headstrong, courageous yet reckless, he charges ahead without a real plan, or serious thought to the consequences. If we connect the characteristics to the person we can say that the subject's lover followed her own desires without much thought to her partner's feelings or to the consequences. Certainly the subject believed this interpretation, adding that she thought her friend had charged over her. But this was the shadow side speaking, the part of her that hurts and wants to blame someone. Without denying this interpretation we must recognize that the card also represents the subject herself.

We can see this fact implied in the presence of such collateral cards as the queen of Swords, and the knight of Cups. If they represent her, then so does the knight of Swords. We can see it in the theme of self so important to this reading. Most important, we can see it in what it tells us about the subject's behaviour. She too charged ahead without thinking of what would happen. She told me that she had pushed for the non-monogamy, assuming somehow that none of their outside affairs would ever amount to anything. When the current situation started she charged over her own feelings, submerging them in the name of being nice to others. And of not admitting her feelings. And now that she had released her emotions she was letting *them* run away with her, going from one extreme to the other, without the balancing calm of Strength. No wonder the Hermit calls her to reflect on what she has done.

The contrast between the knight of Swords and the Hermit can show us how the trump can help counteract the Swords. Where the knight charges, the Hermit stands fixed on his mountain. He grounds himself in wisdom rather than following impulse and desire. Where the knight rides under a stormy sky the Hermit looks down from his place above the clouds. The storm symbolizes confused emotions. The knight believes he can conquer his emotions by willpower, yet we know from the Chariot reversed that the subject has lost the sense of self necessary to focus the will. When we look at the direction of the trees blown by the wind we see that the knight charges directly into the storm. People who get caught up in a cycle of disturbed emotion can become almost attached to the violent passion aroused in such situations. Having lost their balance they need to keep moving or else they will fall over. They must keep talking, keep arguing. In contrast to the knight's constant charge the Hermit accepts silence as a prelude to communication. He climbs above the storm to find a place to stand. At the same time this withdrawal from the battle can work only as a temporary strategy. The problems remain and she must work them out eventually. If she wishes to achieve the queen of Cups she will have to find the strength and will to come down off the mountain. Otherwise she remains with the knight of Cups, an image calmer than the knight of Swords, but ultimately no more satisfying.

We should recognize also that the knight of Swords signifies a desire for battle. Angry at what her partner has done to her, she wants to express her rage. And so she charges, at her partner, the situation, even herself, anything that allows extreme feeling, for any distressing emotion can serve as a vehicle for anger. The knight of Swords resists the Hermit because he believes that the Hermit's calm and peace would mean he has to surrender what he considers his righteous rage. In fact, this fear is illusory. The Hermit does not set preconditions (just as it does not promise solutions). It simply tells her she must return to herself. If she brings anger with her, so be it. She may discover that the anger will settle away when she calms down, but that will happen because she desires it, not because she orders herself to do so.

The knight of Swords is young, untried. The Hermit appears as an old man. When the subject, and her lover, rushed into the situation they did so with naive trust that they could overcome any problems. The Hermit signifies maturity gained through experience. But how real is this maturity? The outcome returns her to the level of a knight.

Finally, where the knight waves his sword, the Hermit leans on his staff. Both signify 'masculine' or mental energy. The knight pushes it outward, towards recklessness and aggressive emotions. The Hermit turns the energy into wisdom, which then becomes a support. At its best the ninth trump develops that wisdom from an underlying 'female' sense of wholeness and mystery. As described above, we see this hidden femininity in the card's position under the High Priestess, in its lunar number, and in the darkness filling the picture. We should notice also that the Hermit looks to the left, traditionally associated with the dark, the feminine, and the instinctive. The knight, in fact, rides to the left, signifying that he gives himself over to emotion. Thus, while both cards display masculine imagery, they carry an underlying femininity, the knight in the feminine's disruptive chaotic form (pushed outwards with masculine force), the Hermit in the sense of endless depth and unity. The contrast between the two can teach us a good deal about the neglected female archetype and how it can be expressed in masculine form.

We have emphasized the knight's recklessness. Before leaving him we should recognize his courage. The subject and her lover had entered new territory, for the most part unexplored and unmapped by the patterns and expectations of culture. They had acted without careful planning, but such planning isn't always possible. And though it had brought them problems problems exist in any relationship. The current divorce rate demonstrates that a code of monogamy does not insure that love will continue or grow. The subject would not help herself if she used this reading only to reject her past decisions. Instead, she needed each image — including the knight's courage — to help her decide what to do now.

The Queen of Swords

After the knight of Swords in the basis came the queen of Swords in the recent past. The subject's recklessness and courage have brought her sorrow, but also wisdom and maturity. We see now that the first step towards the Hermit comes from pain and the shock of seeing what her (and her lover's) knight of Swords attitude has brought them. Her anguish has forced her to look more seriously at what has happened. Notice that the queen looks to the right, in other words, towards rational examination.

The queen sometimes stands for widowhood, and so it emphasizes the subject's recent experience of neglect, aloneness as pain. The movement between 'basis' and 'recent' works very well here. First came the knight's recklessness. From this developed the sense that her partner was ignoring her suffering. And so we see her as a widow. Yet this perception is distorted, for her lover had not left her and did not intend to do so. She had only ignored the subject for a while, an experience which the subject found so uncomfortable she interpreted it as sorrow, even widowhood. The move from the queen in the recent past to the Hermit in the present shows a developing awareness that aloneness can bring strength and self-knowledge. The growth of this awareness into a way of being, the queen of Cups, becomes the task outlined by the reading.

When reversed, the queen of Swords signifies jealousy and aggression. The card here appears right-side up, telling her that her pain is not primarily manipulative. She has not created it in order to get her own way. Because the queen accepts her emotions and works to find wisdom in her experience she has already begun the move towards the Hermit. Where the knight rides beneath the clouds, the queen sits partly above them. In contrast to the Hermit's clear peak the clouds remain as high as her body, but they do not reach the level of her head. The body symbolizes the emotions, the head the intellect. Knowledge and acceptance can lift her from the gloom and anguish she still experiences.

If we set the Hermit vertically then he and the queen look at each other, partners in a way.

Just as the queen looks towards freeing herself through wisdom so the Hermit looks back to the sorrow that created that wisdom. The Hermit contains the queen of Swords within him. If he loses that sense then his knowledge becomes impersonal, masculine in the worst sense of meaning detached from feeling. The Hermit holds a light out to the queen, who opens her left hand to receive it. In her right hand the queen holds the sword of intellect. We should remember that the Hermit's lantern symbolizes teaching as well as personal wisdom. The subject can draw support from such 'outside' sources as the Tarot, books, or her own observation of people.

If the queen extends her hand to the Hermit she looks beyond him as well, to the hand holding out the ace of Swords in the near future. Despite her image of herself as sorrowful she reaches out toward a sense of renewal. And the ace reaches toward her as well, promising a time of new strength and creative energy. Both the queen and the hand from the cloud hold on to something. The queen grasps her sword, symbol of pain and isolation as well as wisdom. The ace changes that to the wand of confidence, emotional strength. Both are alone, but the ace uses aloneness as a source of joy, seeing it as a possibility of development. Because the Hermit, as the crossing card, actually lies horizontally, his staff becomes a bridge between the two hands.

 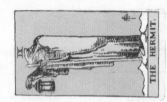 

The Ace of Wands

The staff represents the idea that the ace does not just happen but comes because of the subject's hard work to achieve first some distance from the situation (the Hermit's peak), and second, self-reliance. The blossoming wand shows this attitude becoming reality.

In contrast to the ten dropped wands the Hermit's staff can act as a bridge because he holds on to it. It symbolizes the subject's ability to do something about the problem, rather than throw down her involvement. It also symbolizes the permanent qualities of her life — her own abilities and strength of personality, but also the fixed nature of her relationship with her partner. Even in the image of aloneness, that relationship runs as an underlying current.

In some readings, when a difficult card appears in the near future we remind ourselves of the position's transitory quality. This, too, shall pass. Such a reminder becomes just as important when the card is highly beneficial, especially if it contrasts with other influences or the outcome. Then the subject needs to understand that the pleasant experience will not last and she or he must make the most of it, if possible using it to affect the difficult areas. In this reading the ace, blooming with energy, appears counter to the withdrawn knight of Cups, and especially to the reversed Chariot, Strength, and queen of Cups. The reading tells her she will experience a renewal of confidence, a fresh start, but it will not last. The old patterns and emotions will resurface, unless she can use the ace to change the direction of the reading.

We can see some of the reasons for this temporary quality by comparing the ace to the Hermit. The ace concentrates so much on a new beginning that it tends to forget the difficult and painful process of building up wisdom. It wants to believe that she can put all that behind her and start over. As pure Fire energy the ace lacks the Hermit's focus. It directs itself outward, away from doubts. Optimistic, it loses the Hermit's intimate knowledge of the pessimistic shadow, and without that knowledge optimism cannot carry through to achievement. The ace represents the masculine energy of light in its beneficial aspect of creativity but also in its problem side of ignoring the self in favour of activity. The withdrawn Hermit has struggled with the dark, and through that struggle has become aware of the mystery. He knows the dark as wholeness, as the infinite source of energy which rises to the surface as light and consciousness. The ace of Wands emerges from a cloud of mystery, but optimism ignores the cloud and whatever painful experiences might lie within it. None of this implies that she should ignore the ace or back away from its gift. She needs to use it just because it will not last and there are many areas that can benefit from its fire. The ace is a boost of optimism. But it is not a solution.

The reader will have noticed that we have skipped over the position of possible outcome. In this reading, that position is so bound up with the outcome that we can discuss it best if we wait until the end.

The Chariot (reversed)

The Chariot occupies the position of self. The seventh trump is the archetype of will as a dominating force in life. The reversed Chariot in this position says that the subject lacks the will to continue. At first, I thought that the strains had emptied her of willpower. The actions of other people (her lover and her lover's friend) had so affected her that she lacked the ability, the will, to direct her own life. This over-influence reflected back on the Hermit's call to self-reliance.

Then another interpretation occurred to me. She had overturned the Chariot herself. She had surrendered her will as a way of abrogating responsibility. This was why the card showed up in the position of self. She wanted to get across a certain message to the others: not 'I don't want to continue', but 'I can't continue.' She wanted them to take the step of ending the situation so she could retain her status as a 'nice' person. (We will see a similar mechanism at work with Strength reversed.) In fact, the Chariot reversed does say, 'I don't want to continue.' And it implies, 'I want you to end it. I don't want to have to do it myself.' Therefore she will portray herself *to herself* as lacking enough willpower to push forward. As mentioned above, without the Chariot (7) and Strength (8), the Hermit (9) lacks the support to carry through. The Hermit demands a harsh look at the self. For this too, a lack of will provides an excuse to avoid the experience. Notice that the charioteer holds a magic wand. By reversing the card the subject rejects her own power to find a solution. She would rather remain weak, thereby pushing the others to feel sorrow and guilt for what they have done 'to' her.

When we say that the Chariot represents will, what does that mean? In one sense the Chariot represents a powerful personality that directs life into the pattern it desires. The Charioteer does not resolve the conflicts in his life (symbolized by the black and white sphinxes) but holds them together through the force of his dominant character. Upside-down in this reading, the interpretation tells us that the subject has lost (or given up) the ability to exercise such control over the situation described in the reading. The upside-down Chariot does not necessarily indicate disaster. If will-power means dominance then reversing it can mean allowing things to happen without trying to control them. We will look at this idea of the alternative more closely with Strength.

To some extent the knight of Swords represents a clumsy attempt at the domineering side of the Chariot. Just as he charges *into* situations without foresight, so he also charges *at* them, trying to make things come out the way he wants. But the knight is young, and part of his courage is arrogance. The movement to the queen has brought the subject a painful wisdom. The Chariot reversed could indicate that she will give up the knight's attempt to overpower problems and find some other approach. If she can no longer hold the sphinxes together by force of will then maybe she will find some way to reconcile them. However, she must choose to do this. The loss of will by itself cannot take her to the next step of seeking something else.

In this interpretation the presence of Strength reversed becomes a crucial factor. Coming directly after the Chariot, the eighth trump symbolizes that other way of handling life's problems and especially the emotions. As either a fear or a hope, Strength reversed can prove dangerous to somebody with the Chariot reversed in the position of self. It leaves her without resources.

Overthrowing the Chariot becomes a possible benefit if we see 'will-power' as a kind of force. But we can also look at will as acting and directing your life from the centre of your being, calling upon all your faculties to deal with the world. The seventh card bears allusions to each of the six cards preceding it, from the Magician's wand in the Charioteer's hand to the lingam and yoni sign representing the Lovers on the front of the Chariot. He has assimilated these qualities into himself.

Such an inner power does not come easily. Few people achieve it in any complete way. Still, we can work with this image in exercises and meditations as a way of calling up will-power as something from inside rather than something imposed mentally. If we see the Chariot in this way in this reading, then reversed means that the subject lacks the inner resource to deal with her problems. The Hermit calls her to return to wholeness and from there to climb the mountain of self awareness. To do so, she must find — create — the will to do so. When we look at the many ambiguities of Strength reversed we will see some of the reasons for this lack (surrender) of will. At the same time we will see how the male Chariot and female Strength do not really oppose each other, as conflicting approaches, but work together, feeding each other, to produce the unified (androgynous) power of the Hermit.

The Three of Cups
Before Strength we come to the three of Cups. As mentioned above, I expected to see it in a reading on this subject. Sometimes specific cards or configurations in a reading will appear so fascinating to the reader that he or she must suppress a desire to nod in acknowledgement, or say something like 'I thought so', or even laugh at the steadfastness of old friends like the three of Cups. For the reader the cards stimulate the mind and the instincts. For the subject, however, they describe a moment in a life.

In this reading the three of Cups reversed described the atmosphere between the three people as a group. They had lost their cohesiveness and ease with each other. The subject told me that they all used to do things together as friends, but that this closeness had fallen off in recent weeks, largely because of the subject herself. She did not feel great antagonism toward her partner's friend — she directed most of her anger at her partner — but she found herself uncomfortable with the two of them together, as if she was encouraging them against her own best interests.

Because the card appears in her reading it describes her perceptions, her discomfort, along with the fact that the three were not as close as they once had been. This subjectivity became clearer several days later when the subject told me about the reading the other two had done that day, where the three of Cups came in the position of possible outcome. The two readings do not contradict each other; instead, they show different perspectives.

Beyond the three people directly involved, the reversed three of Cups can apply to a general lack of support the subject found in her environment. Many of her friends thought the whole thing was wrong and should stop. Though they meant well, they isolated the subject because their attitude made it difficult for her to ask for advice or even emotional support. Looking beyond to the social climate the subject said that she and the others often felt weighed down by the traditional assumptions about couples and outside relationships. The vast number of movies and books in which people separate or even murder each other because of adultery reminded the subject that they had entered unexplored areas and would have to find their own way.

Strength (reversed)

The Chariot reversed in 'self' indicated that the subject lacks will. But she fears (and hopes for) the loss of her inner strength. The eighth trump in the position of hopes and fears is pivotal in this reading. The blocks symbolized by the card are just those which hamper the subject from dealing successfully with the problems and emerging as her goal, the queen of Cups. And because it occupies a position of expectations rather than something already established, it throws the development back on her. As with many cards, especially the vital ones in a reading, Strength here symbolizes a whole complex of qualities, a whole range of states feared and desired. In our discussion we looked closely at this last aspect, that she hoped for Strength reversed as well as fearing it. To some extent the fear comes from the hope; because she thinks she's not supposed to hope for weakness (or resentment) she shifts the conscious emotion into fear. This way she can stay focused on the expectation and help bring it about while pretending to herself that she wants to avoid it. The reading helps bring this to her attention. It doesn't so much tell her something she doesn't know as help her to face something she doesn't want to recognize. Also, because the information comes in the form of a symbol she can work directly with that symbol to change her attitude.

As the first card of the second line of seven, Strength occupies the same position as the Magician in the first line. It begins the task of the second line, which is that of exploring the inner world of the self. The Hermit, with its withdrawal from the outside world and its mental alertness, starts the process of exploration. But the first step is finding, or summoning, the inner strength to carry the process through. Just as the Hermit adds masculine qualities to the High Priestess's sense of lunar mystery, so Strength brings a feminine acceptance to the solar power of the Magician. It implies a recognition of your own power, an ease with your passions. It allows you to bring up feelings and desires and to cope with them — peacefully, joyously. The subject fears she will lack this quality. She desires that lack as well. Since

Strength implies acceptance she makes the subconscious connection, 'If I have the strength to accept the situation then I will have to accept it. If I'm too weak and can't handle it, then they'll have to break up, and it won't be my fault.' Strength does not actually require her to accept something she finds damaging. It does, however, put the responsibility back on her. She cannot hide behind weakness.

Similarly, to look at things peacefully might imply not looking at them furiously. If she has absorbed the idea that anger is not nice, that she shouldn't express rage, then as a strong person she would expect herself to overcome such bad feelings. On the other hand, weak people can do what they want because they cannot help themselves. In fact, anger, suppressed violence and various other 'unacceptable' emotions are part of the inner material brought out and accepted in Strength. Only, the card shows them surfacing through the power of love, self love as much as the love of others. Gently the woman closes the lion's mouth, taming the wild passions through acceptance.

Here we come to a wonderful illustration of the psyche's ability to hold two contradictory positions at the same time, and to express both in the same symbol. The symbol *means* the contradiction as well as the specific sides producing it. We have seen that she desires a lack of strength because weakness gives her the excuse to indulge anger. At the same time she fears Strength because genuine Strength *does* allow her to express anger. Now, this is complicated. It says, on the one hand, that Strength implies giving up anger, and on the other hand the acting out of anger. Both are true, partly because the acting out of anger allows you to to get over it. She wants to keep her anger, to hoard it, let it build, like a miser. And so she hopes for weakness. Even if we couldn't reconcile the two positions, even if we couldn't make the neat formula: give up your anger by expressing it, the mind could still keep the two positions and still express both by the same symbol with equal conviction. We only see these things as a contradiction when we bring them to the surface. Then we can decide whether to try for a resolution or let the different attitudes continue.

Strength stresses acceptance rather than struggle, being rather than doing. It forms a partnership with the Hermit, the card after it. In a reading where the two appear together Strength implies acceptance as a step towards the Hermit's maturity and responsibility.

If Strength symbolizes taming the passions then such an idea can easily become confused with controlling or repressing passion, especially anger. Looked at this way, reversed Strength becomes the hope/desire of not holding in her rage. She fears really letting it out, she fears losing control, not just of 'bad' feelings, but also of her own sense of well being. For Strength implies a different aspect of that same self-reliance we saw in her partner, the Hermit. In Strength it surfaces as confidence, trust, happiness. She fears losing these things by losing control.

The Chariot represented strength of character, as expressed in a powerful will. At the end of its line it stands for the culmination of that approach to life. The eighth trump, beginning a new line, begins a new approach as well — a yielding, soft kind of strength that doesn't impose itself on others or on the world, but allows people to be and events to happen. In some readings we see a recommendation for one of these approaches in place of the other. This reading contains both, with neither fulfilled. It reminds us that they complement each other, and that the Chariot comes first. It can take a strong will to surrender to a situation without believing that surrender implies defeat. The lack of will in the position of self makes it harder to look for Strength as an expectation. And vice versa, for she fears not having the Strength to direct her will towards choice and positive development.

So far we have looked at passion in terms of rage. But the lion symbolizes sexuality as well, and Strength reversed indicates her fear that her lover's action will drain away her own sexuality. To some extent this idea comes from cultural tradition which depicts the cuckold as impotent, the 'betrayed' wife as frigid. Most people find it hard to shake off such encrusted images, even if they do not believe in the attitudes behind them. It becomes especially difficult when it reinforces a personal reaction, such as feelings of rejection, of not being good enough sexually. The subject told me that intellectually she never believed a person could only love or desire one person at a time. She believed it natural for people to direct their sexuality at various objects without losing their original feelings. During her own outside relationships she often found that her desire for her partner increased because the lion had become more active and that activity came home with her. And yet, when her partner became involved with someone new the subject could not shake the belief that her own sexual lack had somehow caused this to happen. Strength reversed represents this fear, as well as the fear of lacking the strength to overcome such ideas.

Because people focus so sharply on sexuality the image of it works as a metaphor for a person's whole way of being in the world. When we describe a man as 'virile' or 'potent' we do not mean his performance in bed or his ability to engender children. The loss of sexual strength means the loss of creativity, of confidence, of power in general. The subject fears their loss and she blames her partner's affair. The Tarot does not assure her that the fear is groundless. The difficulty of this reading (and of many similar readings) comes from its refusal to make specific statements about the future of the relationship or even the current conditions. Instead, it tells her to look to herself. It does not remove the fear but it describes it for what it is — a fear rather than an established fact. It puts it back where it belongs, in the subject's anxieties instead of in the outside world. And it allows her to see some of the causes of that fear in her desire for weakness.

The Knight of Cups

We have already looked at several facets of the knight of Cups. In a significant reading we will very often understand the final card before we get to it. It may seem almost inevitable as the sum of the previous cards. We have considered the knight of Cups as an advance over the knight of Swords, and as a reflection of the failure to achieve the queen of Cups. And we have described it as a (lesser) reflection of the Hermit. By itself, the card means a person who is calm, withdrawn, yet feels a pressure from outside. He tends towards passivity, and self-absorption, but as a knight he cannot neglect his sense of duty to others. We see him riding to the right, as if he returns to rationality and outside obligations. But in comparison to the knight of Swords' wild rush to emotionalism (to the left) he rides very slowly, wishing to stay as long as possible within himself. The card indicates a reluctance by the subject to deal with the issues and problems raised. She wants to separate herself, not let the others bother her any more. She feels she has given too much of herself already. The outcome card shows a new facet of the environment. Not just the bad feeling, or the lack of support, but also the subject's own rejection of involvement. The knight of Cups knows he must return to responsibility, but he wants everyone to leave him alone.

We can see how this attitude distorts the Hermit. The trump withdraws for a purpose, to regain a sense of the self and its resources. The knight wants to stay in the cool darkness because he finds it more pleasant. In doing so, however, he begins to lose touch with that powerful sense of being found in the Hermit. The river of the unconscious flows through the card but does not touch the knight whose horse stands on bare ground. Trees grow on the other side of the river. Only by crossing the water, that is, returning to involvement, can she attach herself to life.

At the beginning of this reading we saw how the subject's personal iconography included the knight and the queen of Cups. Previously she had used the knight as her significator. She saw the queen as a symbol of her goals in life. Therefore, the knight as outcome shows a regression, an immature approach compared to the Hermit's maturity. Instead of using the experience to go forward in life, to the queen of Cups, she lets it become a setback.

The knight of Swords also represented a specific person. The subject's partner used it as her significator. If that card as basis showed her too much under the influence of her partner's actions, then the knight of Cups does suggest a return to autonomy. If only she could bring the queen to its fulfilled aspect she could realize the possibilities of the upright knight. For the knight of Cups does not oppose the queen. The one develops naturally from the other. Only, she must make that development happen, she must want it to happen, and we have seen in the Chariot and Strength how a side of her prefers weakness.

Something very interesting occurs if we compare the movement of the knight of Swords to the queen of Swords with the knight of Cups to the queen of Cups reversed. The first happens almost without effort. Recklessness brings pain. She may have to strive for the wisdom involved, but the pain comes easily. By contrast the much more desirable queen of Cups does not emerge from the knight. To reach that development will require a struggle, with herself and possibly with others. Why should life bring sorrow as a matter of course, while demanding of us that we wrestle with ourselves and the world for happiness? I think the Tarot, and this reading in particular, suggests an answer. Struggle contains its own value. If joy came to us with the same ease as pain, we would never feel any pressure towards consciousness or self-knowledge, we would not develop will, or the inner strength to yield and accept what we cannot overpower. Life rigs the game against us so that we play harder. Of course, this idea assumes purpose in the universe, and we cannot prove such an assumption. Still, we can demonstrate — and the Tarot helps us demonstrate — that life operates in this way.

The queen of Cups does not represent happiness so much as fulfilment. Like the angel in Temperance and the woman in the Star she combines the imagery of land and water. Her throne sits on the earth, but the water flows into her dress. She acts in the world without losing the inner awareness that gives her action meaning. The subject told me that she saw the card as a goal because the queen symbolizes a powerful personality who does not seek to dominate but directs herself toward creativity. She holds an elaborate cup in her hand, her own creation (according to Waite's description) and she looks at it with fierce intensity, seeking further inspiration from what she's already accomplished. The subject originally switched from the knight of Cups to the queen of Wands at her lover's suggestion. She kept it because of a strong fire influence in her horoscope and because it reflected her basic optimism in two directions: inward to greater self-knowledge and confidence, outward to achievement and success.

As a queen, the card implies female Strength, with its gentle power. As a card of the will manifesting itself in the world it calls up the Chariot. The Hermit took a basically masculine approach to the feminine mystery of being. The queen of Cups applies a feminine sense of life to the masculine activity of achievement.

Her will derives from something more than inner force. All her activity generates from love. Love for others, love for herself, love of the world and its possibilities. The card brings us to the realization that only in love can we find the strength and will to create something of value in our lives. Therefore, the queen of Cups reversed signifies more than a failure of self development. It stands for a failure of love. In the series of meditations described below the subject discovered this for herself when she sought to enter the card and to bring it within herself. We will look at this experience in a moment. Here we should remember that like the three of Pentacles in a previous reading the presence of the queen signifies the potential of its achievement. Reversed, it indicates the likely failure of that achievement. Seeing it, however, recognizing its value, the subject can work consciously towards its fulfilment.

Before looking at the meditation pattern that came out of this reading we should look briefly at three of the cards from the other reading done that day. As mentioned above, when the subject's partner and her friend laid the cards, the three of Cups appeared, right-side up, in the position of possible outcome. The two central cards also reflected the subject's readings. They were the Moon crossed by the nine of Pentacles.

Both these cards reflect different sides of the Hermit. First, however, we need to go back to that three of Cups. It did not contradict the subject's reading, which showed it reversed in the environment. That reading showed the state of things at the moment. When she told me about this parallel reading the subject also told me how the others were conscious of the loss of closeness between the three of them. In her own reading, however, she concentrated on this loss as a lack of support, whereas the others shifted the card to the realm of possibility, where they could optimistically hope of restoring it to its

upright position. Notice that a card of three people showed up, rather than, say, the two of Cups signifying a new relationship. Neither of these women wanted the original relationship to break up and a new primary relationship to form. Instead, they look to a solution of love and trust between the three of them. Whether they can achieve this remains open.

The central card, the Moon, symbolizes deep fears rising to the surface. We have seen how the Hermit follows the lunar path of mystery. At the same time he approaches it through rationality and the development of wisdom. In the eighteenth trump the Moon takes over completely so that the person loses the Hermit's solid ground, and in fact, the recognizable human personality disappears, replaced by instinctive 'animal' responses. This is why the Moon card shows no human figures. As the card of the centre the Moon emphasized the fear the women felt facing an unknown situation. Some of this fear had been suppressed for the sake of a positive outlook. Now, in a crisis time, the anxieties rushed up to the surface.

The nine of Pentacles crossed the Moon. Since this card primarily means discipline the women saw it as a way of dealing with fear and with the situation as a whole. They must not give in to anxiety, or jealousies, but must discipline the mind to its more developed possibilities. The woman who laid the cards — the 'third woman' from our subject's point of view — saw the position of crossing card as a 'bridge' to the possible outcome. In other words, through consciously directing themselves in positive directions, and not giving in to fear or anger or pessimism they could work towards making the three of Cups a reality.

Discipline does not imply repression. The bird is hooded, not caged. Symbolic of the mind, the imagination, the spirit, the falcon follows the will of the dedicated woman who has trained it. Like the Hermit (also nine) the card contains aspects of Strength and the Chariot. Discipline allows the hidden fears and passions to emerge, but uses them to strengthen the will.

If we consider this card as part of 'our' reading, then another aspect becomes important. The picture shows a woman alone. This returns us to the theme of self-reliance. In order to deal with the situation she (each one) must become her own person. The subject in particular must give up the tendency to look to weakness as a means of getting the others to remove the problems. And more. She can use the situation, difficult as it is, to further her own sense of self. In the frame of mind shown in the nine of Pentacles any strong experience can become a joy. This is the mind of the hunter, whose falcon is the soul, and whose prey is life.

The woman in the nine of Pentacles has created herself. And she has done it alone (compare the card to the Lovers, where two people together bring forth the angel). But the card's position in its reading describes it as a bridge to the three of Cups. Through true discipline, through each one's reliance on herself, the three women can come together.

Like the Hermit, the woman in the nine of Cups implies an androgyny. In the trump we saw a male figure, symbolic of rationality and discernment. He applied these qualities to a female awareness of mystery and wisdom. Here in the nine we see a woman in a garden — both images suggest a yielding to life's pleasures. She achieves this state of union with life through discipline, traditionally seen as a masculine value. But this view looks on discipline only in terms of control and obedience. The discipline of the stern father, imposed from above on his children. Discipline as a positive force requires a merging with the female qualities of wildness and intense love of life. Out of this tension comes the creation of self.

THE FIRST MEDITATION

These ideas and themes from the other reading did not come until later, when the subject discussed them with her partner and then with me. At the time, working with her reading alone, we looked at the question of how to counteract its weaknesses and the pessimistic outlook shown in the reversed cards, particularly the queen of Cups. The reading itself helps by bringing attitudes to consciousness and showing her what she needs. But she wanted a way to use the reading to take positive steps.

One method is meditation with the images. Each of the pictures represents a whole complex of experiences and expectations. By entering them a person can act on the complex at the level of its symbol. Meditation allows the subject to overcome a certain passivity in the face of the influences shown in the reading. It helps develop free will. Many people, when looking at a reading take the attitude, 'Now that I've seen where it's going I don't have to allow it.' The situation is not so simple. A reading shows powerful tendencies, and we cannot counteract them just by saying so. The true exercise of free will requires an effort. Meditation helps us focus desire.

We set up what I call a 'mandala'. Simple in form, it consisted of her significator in the centre with the Hermit beneath her, the queen of Cups above, and the Chariot and Strength on the sides.

QUEEN of CUPS.

THE CHARIOT.

QUEEN of WANDS.

STRENGTH.

THE HERMIT.

From the beginning the mandala says that she will not accept the upside-down cards. She will turn them upright and work with them in their fulfilled aspects. We chose these particular ones and left out others, especially the three of Cups, so that she could concentrate on herself without feeling obligated to think of the others. Using a group of cards does not mean that she must keep all of them in her mind all the time. She can experience them as a pattern, or focus on just one card, or some particular relationship, or pay no attention to them at all but allow them to seep into her.

The form gives two axes, a vertical, consisting of the Hermit rising to the queen, and a horizontal one of the Chariot and Strength, in which the energy moves back and forth between them. Both axes contain movement and for both, her own card, the queen of Wands, rests in the centre.

This structure raises some interesting questions about the Celtic cross itself. In many books on the Tarot instructions for the Celtic cross include ritual descriptions of each position. 'This is beneath her' (basis); 'This is above her' or 'This crowns her' (possible outcome); 'This is behind her' (recent past); 'This is before her' (near future). When I began working with the Celtic cross I tended to discard these phrases, looking instead for the inner content of the position. Through this and other meditations, however (my own as well as those I've given to others) I have found myself returning to these descriptions, not as a ritual, but as a symbol. To call the Hermit 'beneath' her places it in a context of something within, already accomplished but hidden, so that she needs to bring it from beneath — the unconscious — to the centre — consciousness. The queen of Cups is 'above' her, something she wishes to achieve, to reach for. But the movement has to begin below, with the Hermit, and the way passes through herself in the centre, with her knowledge of who she is, independent of whatever archetype she passes through. Beneath and above form an axis of becoming. In mythological terms it reaches from the underworld of hidden experience to the god-lands of spiritual development.

The cards 'behind' and 'before' form a horizontal axis — events in the real world, experiences which happen to the person. We do not see this so much in the mandala pattern as in the reading itself. She went through the queen of Swords and she will go through the ace of Wands. Both affect her, but neither one lasts. If we look at the horizontal axis of the meditation we see that the Chariot and Strength represent archetypal forces she needs to find in herself, but they do not call her to become their images in the way of the two vertical cards. On either side, they balance and support her, but she remains the centre.

As the first step I told the subject to balance the cards from the centre in a way that represented the balance in herself. After some experimenting she set them up in the following way.

The Hermit overlapped her because she felt it close to her. The queen of Cups seemed distant yet powerful, and so she placed it above, remote yet strong enough to lift her beyond herself. Similarly she could not feel the Chariot and Strength as close to her, and she placed them away, at the same time feeling that the distance actually increased their power, like weights at the end of a long fulcrum.

I suggested to her that she do five meditations, and asked if she would keep a record of her reactions and discoveries. Since we discussed in detail her experiences I have put them in my own words, along with some observations of my own about the general implications of her discoveries.

I suggested also that she work with light and darkness as ways of approaching the inner qualities of the cards. In terms of meditation, light and dark are not concepts or metaphors but direct experiences. We imagine the body as filled with light in each breath, or else we feel ourselves descend into darkness. The light lifts us from our difficulties. It drains away the leaden weight of problems and allows us to love by cleansing the heart.

Darkness takes us into the silence and mystery of being. In darkness we free ourselves from the distractions of the outside world. This experience is very different from the fear and shock we saw in the darkness of the nine of Swords. There the repressed emotions rose up to overwhelm. In the darkness of the Hermit, which is the darkness of the High Priestess, we sink below agitation to the still centre.

Some people find this approach difficult, especially if they've taken meditation classes which taught them to join themselves entirely to light. To some extent such teachings arise from the long patriarchal tradition linking light — maleness — good, and dark — femaleness — evil. Denied, darkness becomes fear. Frightening images do hide within each of us. The last seven cards of the Major Arcana take us into these areas as shown in the Devil, the Moon, and Judgement. Yet life itself, as well as knowledge and inspiration, emerges from darkness, and it is possible to join ourselves to that lifegiving wholeness without stirring up personal anxieties or primal terrors. Because the subject had studied with me she understood what I meant when I told her to 'work with light and darkness'.

We did not discuss any time limit for the meditations. At first the subject thought to do them on consecutive days. After the first two, however, she found it better to space them out, giving herself a chance to work them through as well as to think about the reading and try to apply it in her life. At the time of this writing she had done four and had decided to postpone the final one until the moment seemed right.

She began the first meditation by switching the Chariot and Strength, so that Strength was on the left, the 'female' or instinctive side. (Later on she noticed that the queen of Wands held her staff in the hand on the left — like the Charioteer's wand — and a flower — like the flowery wreath of Strength — on the right.) After a moment of fixing the pattern in her mind she decided to turn off the lights. (When we are most attuned to light and dark the outside environment hardly affects us. But if we find ourselves blocked then altering the surroundings can sometimes help.) A curious thing then happened. She turned off the lights in the room where she'd gone to meditate but decided to leave the hall light on in case her friend should come home. A curtain separated the two rooms, and she pulled it shut, but when she sat down before the cards she discovered that she'd left the curtain open just enough for a single shaft of light to come through. And this light fell exactly on the card of Strength and nowhere else.

By such tricks the unconscious gets our attention. She moved all the cards into the light, but when she began her meditation, moving between light and dark, she became aware of Strength as a card of light, and the Chariot as a card of darkness. For even though the Chariot is a male image, and we think of will as a masculine function, it emerges from the centre of a person's being. And while we can infuse that centre with light it belongs by nature to the creative dark. Strength, the card 'below' the Magician, lives in the light, for it is a card of expressing joy.

Through the meditation she became aware of the simplest meanings of the Chariot and Strength. The Chariot signified the desire and intention to go ahead, see the thing through. This intention, stated to herself and not just to the others, was of great importance. It helped her go beyond some of the ambivalence of the ten of Wands. She needed to know that she herself wished to go forward. Strength then became the quality of actually doing it. And, as I pointed out to her when we discussed it, because a clear realization of will dispels doubt it releases strength as well as requiring it.

THE SECOND MEDITATION

The second meditation occurred a few days later. As she laid out the cards she began noticing correspondences. A river appears in both the queen of Cups and the Chariot. Where the river flows into the queen's dress the Chariot separates itself from the water. Will derives from the centre but the act of imposing it on the world can cut us off from its source in the unconscious.

In the first meditation she had thought of Strength as light. Now she noticed that while both Strength and the queen of Wands are solar cards (the lion symbolizes the sun, Wands is the suit of Fire) both are women. They represent a feminine appreciation of solar optimism and love of life.

Another realization came to her as she began the meditation itself. The Hermit and the queen of Cups are both androgynous, but the queen realizes a fuller integration of the two sides. She begins with an inner peace and then extends this to action in the world. The Hermit must struggle for female wisdom (wholeness) by first renouncing the world of action and then by using the male principle of acquisition to acquire understanding, to conquer the self.

What is it about the self that needs to be conquered? Is it simply destructive (or embarrassing) emotions, such as jealousy, anger, weakness, and the desire for weakness? Perhaps it's both more and less. The idea of the Hermit can lead us to a sense of climbing above the personality mask that we create as our way of being in the world. This gives us a sense of overcoming qualities that may seem to cling to us against our will. At the same time, from that peak above the storm we can safely bring out the so called negative emotions and realize that these too express real moods belonging to a person's life. In her identification with the Hermit the subject saw again how she could allow all these troubled selves to emerge, and without passing moralist judgement on them — this feeling is good, this one is bad. She could use them, use the lion's energy to become free of automatic or controlled responses. From this state, from the Hermit beneath her, she can move to the queen of Cups above. For the queen goes beyond freedom to action.

While both the Hermit and the queen of Cups embody the feminine (from opposite directions — the Hermit embraces the female in the wise old man manner, while the queen arises out of it) neither is passive. Both struggle with life and their own being. Their purpose is to create the self, to bring it into the world. Only the knight of Cups represents passivity in this reading. By resisting involvement it blocks the passage from the Hermit to the queen. By leaving it out of her mandala — and by turning upright the reversed cards — she breaks through the blocks, or bypasses them to create a new situation.

While the above observations came spontaneously to the subject during her meditation I have elaborated them out of the discussion we had when she described her experiences to me. The following points come directly from her report. In her meditation she used breathing to move between light and darkness. With each in breath she filled herself with light. On the out-breath she released all the light, letting it carry away her thoughts. In this way she made room for the darkness. Doing this she became aware that she was seeking to awaken the darkness — stir the inner mystery to life.

Becoming comfortable with darkness meant becoming comfortable with aloneness. The Hermit finds support within herself, not from other people or social approval. It reminded her of the need to find something valuable for herself in the situation, something that would equal the 'profit' her partner got from having a second relationship. And she needed to find it in aloneness. In this way she would go beyond the altruism of doing things solely for other people.

In her breathing she moved from light to dark. But she also moved from Strength to the Chariot, which became for her a sense of moving from a potential to realization, or in other words, putting what she had learned from the reading into her life. And finally, her breathing gave her an awareness of the movement from being to doing, a paradox, since physically it moved from light to dark.

At the end of the meditation, as a gesture of humility to the hidden sources of understanding and knowledge she bent forward to touch her forehead to the floor. Without any conscious plan she discovered that her head touched the card of the Hermit.

THE THIRD MEDITATION

Despite the many realizations that came to her in these two meditations she felt herself blocked. The cards' meanings had greatly expanded for her, and she became more conscious of her own needs and desires, but she could not bring the dark over herself, could not find the Hermit's peace. Nor did the light flow easily. At other times, when she had done this sort of meditation with me in a class, she would fill herself with air from the diaphragm to the top of the chest, and the air would fill with light, so that when she released it the dark would rise naturally. But now, the breathing stopped halfway and with it the light, and even if she expelled her breath forcefully she could not empty herself to allow the inside to open. A murkiness seemed to fill her and she could not get past it. At first she identified the cause of this problem as a barrier of tension, anxiety, anger, like a kind of layer coating her and preventing her from penetrating into herself. Later she thought how she had seen the need for finding a value in her aloneness but had not yet done so. In her third meditation she focused on her breathing. There was 'no movement' as she put it. The centre remained closed. She could not enter it from above, or rise up from beneath it.

THE FOURTH MEDITATION

In the fourth meditation she again found herself blocked. Now, however, she decided to take a more active approach to the cards. Instead of working with the three trumps as a way of reaching the queen of Cups she went directly to that card. At first she felt as closed to it as before. But I had suggested to her that she try holding it in her hand or pressing it against her body. Overcoming a slight self-consciousness she picked it up and held it in her lap.

Our minds do not exist in some void outside our bodies. In bringing the body into the meditation we become part of the symbol. All the queens partake partly of the Great Mother, whose love fills the world and the lives of her children. And one of the Mother's enduring images is that of holding her child in her lap — Christ held by Mary, Isis enfolding pharaoh. But now the subject had placed the Mother in *her* lap, thereby becoming the symbol herself. And so she allowed herself to love, and to remember that love is the key to the queen of Cups. Through love the queen develops the intense will shown in the way she stares at her cup. Through love she can act without losing the flow of her inner life. With the queen of Cups in her lap the subject found herself able to love her partner and the 'other' woman, who was still her own friend. For those moments she loved them without thought of benefit or reward.

The experience did not remove all her blocks. Nor did she feel she could repeat it on demand. It did, however, show her something of the way to continue.

After the meditation she decided to wait before doing the fifth. Partly she wanted time to assimilate some of the experiences and thoughts brought out in the first four. And partly she wanted the fifth to act in some way as a culmination. This required her to wait for the proper moment. The fact that she felt she could do this showed that her confidence had grown. She could let herself grow toward the queen of Cups. She had not abandoned her meditation series but only suspended it so that a certain sharpness would stay alive in her. Under the surface of patience she could continue to move.

Though she put off her final meditation she did do one more exercise using the pattern. Bothered by that murkiness she decided to try a meditation with the Hermit. She laid out the whole pattern, and since the Hermit carries a staff she laid beside her a straight tree branch she had found while walking in a wood near her home. When she had gone through her preparations, feeling again that denseness that kept her outside herself, she picked up the Hermit. Now, one way to join the dark is through a 'descent' — imagining yourself going downwards, for we envision darkness as below. She had tried this before, without result. This time she took the card and moved it down and then away from her body. Almost immediately she experienced a cleaning out of her body, and with it a sense of descending further and further into herself, finding a place untouched by the presence of the outside. In her mind, meanwhile, she kept an image of wholeness, and a sense of humility, so she would not allow her ego to take over with pride at how well she was accomplishing her meditation. After a time the movement became so powerful she knew she must stop, so she put down the card, and picked up the branch, holding it upright against her body, and envisioning it as connecting the outside world and consciousness to that deep place she'd found within herself (this image comes partly from a workshop exercise she had done with me). Afterwards she looked again at the card and saw the Hermit's staff as more than a symbol of wisdom. It symbolized as well the true vertical axis, leading from the great above to the great below, and back again.

In describing this woman's report of her meditation I want to stress that the card did not possess her or contain some inherent power to awaken magical forces in her. The power lay in the symbol's articulation of experience. Because she understood something of the states implied in the pictures she understood as well that the card embodied them in a physical form which she could use as an aid. If someone who did not understand Tarot or meditation picked up the Hermit it is highly unlikely that any movement would occur. This does not imply that all experience comes from the imagination. The Tarot, like other esoteric systems of thought, insists that it describes objective fact. But it only links us to those facts, and even if we use the cards as a bridge, they are not the facts themselves, but only a special kind of description, one which describes more and more the more we explore them.

At the time of this writing the subject still had not done the final meditation. At the same time she had not stopped thinking about the reading, or drawing on its images for support and direction. More important, she did not, like the reading itself, seek any predictions as to whether or not the situation between the three of them would work out. She had learned from the reading that she did not need to push herself or manipulate the others towards one solution or another. Instead, she tried to know her own mind, and her own needs, and keep them clear as she struggled for Strength, and will, and love.

Chapter 3.

The Work Cycle

The Celtic cross serves primarily as a description. It lays out the different aspects of a person's situation, sometimes with astonishing complexity. Many people, however, find that it leaves them uncertain of where to go next. Several years ago I decided to develop a spread that would look primarily at what a person needed to do to deal with whatever situation she or he was facing. I called this the 'work cycle', 'work' because it showed what to do, and 'cycle' because if the first seven cards do not give a clear picture you can lay out another line, or 'cycle', beneath them, and another one beneath that. Theoretically up to ten lines are possible, but I have never found it necessary to go beyond three. The form, lines of seven, derives from the Major Arcana, with its three rows, or three levels, of seven cards each. (For a fuller description of this connection see *Seventy-Eight Degrees of Wisdom, Part Two.*)

The layout and positions are as follows. The reader and the subject choose the significator, and the subject shuffles the cards, in the same way as with the Celtic cross. Then the reader sets down a cover card, and a crossing card, also very similar to the cross. The work cycle, however, emphasizes the idea that the crossing card derives from the basic situation shown in the first. Below this configuration the reader lays down a line of seven cards, with the middle card directly under the cross. The first two cards form what I call the 'preparation'. The first represents past experience, and is similar to the 'basis' in the Celtic cross. The second I call 'expectations'. Similar to 'hopes and fears' it shows what development the person expects from the situation.

The middle three cards go together, as the 'work'. They show the forces/possibilities/conditions the person can use or must overcome.

They enable the subject to look at the reading from the standpoint of 'What can I do?' Originally I gave each one a position. In practice I have found it more valuable to leave them open. Most often the meanings combine in some way.

The final two cards represent 'outcome' and 'result'. While the sixth card shows what's likely to happen under the current influences — the same as the 'outcome' in the Celtic cross — the seventh indicates how the person will react to this development. Therefore, instead of ending with the outcome the reading carries it a step further by throwing the emphasis back on the person.

WORK CYCLE ONE

This reading arose out of a crisis situation. Some time before the reading the subject had formed a close friendship with a woman who was severely depressed, and in fact, suicidal. The two of them had become very isolated, as the subject tried to help her friend, and the friend depended more and more on her. While the subject did not actively try to dissuade the woman from her ultimate goal, she did try to open the possibility to her that life held some hope. Instead, the pressure led to a minor breakdown and a destructive (though not serious) act against her own body. When she recovered she moved to another country where she involved herself in living. She made new friends, found work and a place to live, she re-opened dormant interests in such things as art and music, she did some teaching in Eastern medicine, a study she had done before the period of isolation.

Then her friend sent her a letter. They had not lost touch. They wrote regularly to each other, though each letter tended to leave the subject distressed for several days. Now, however, the friend wrote that she wanted to visit the subject in her new home. She made it clear as well that she had not gone beyond her depression or her fixation with suicide.

The subject came for a reading not knowing what to do, not even sure what she wanted. She cared for this person and did not feel she could just abandon her to her own agonies. At the same time she herself did not want to return to the earlier situation. She saw her new home as a new beginning. If her friend came would that contaminate her new life with the past? Since she clearly needed advice we decided to do a work cycle reading. For significator we chose the queen of Pentacles, a card which stressed the new joy she'd found in her daily life.

The crossing cards were Death and the knight of Pentacles.

After some sixteen years of Tarot reading I still find myself astonished at times by the cards' ability to speak so directly to a situation. Writers on Tarot (myself included) often stress that Death does not refer to someone dying, but rather to transformation, a concept sometimes reduced to a cliché I refer to as death-of-the-old-self. Certain of Death's marvellous qualities, people become immured to the fact that the card is called death, and that death means a final ending of something The transformation in fact comes afterward, in Temperance. Death is the clearing away, and the experience can be a painful loss, for even if we know the time has come to change we still cling to the habits and structures that have shaped our lives.

But in this reading Death is literal. Not anyone dying, but the *idea* of death. As the centre card it tells her that the reading does not concern moral responsibility or practical choices. It concerns death. The desire to die. The presence of death in the form of a woman who seeks suicide as an answer to life. It is not just her friend or her own sense of loyalty the subject must confront, but death itself, the lure and the beauty of it.

When younger, she told me, she herself had battled against depression. She felt she could help the other because of her own experience. Even now, the world would sometimes empty out for her, losing all meaning and belief. Knowing someone who embraced death, even theoretically, held a fascination for her. In her new city, her new activities, she had committed herself to life. Or so she thought. But now that fascination threatened to invade this new life, bringing along everything she thought she had left behind.

And Death is fascinating. He comes forward as a conqueror, arrogant, all powerful. Usually, in considering this card, we think of Death as a merciful law of change, sweeping away rigid attitudes, symbolized by the fallen king. But this reading makes us remember the terrible power of death, the only absolute fact in our lives. The only thing that cannot slide away, the only thing that never compromises, that never loses. And so Death attracts us, overwhelms with an almost sexual power. In this one card, the reading forces the subject to look at her own ambivalence to death. It makes her realize that she has tried to push that ambivalence away by coming to a new place and starting new activities. As we shall see in a moment with the knight of Pentacles, she thought she had made a fresh beginning, but in fact had placed outside developments as a barrier against the power of death. Now, death was demanding her attention. She needed to recognize her attraction to it and at the same time decide what practical steps to take.

That decision depended in part on how she dealt with the attraction. In order to decide whether or not she could see her friend again, she needed to know something of her own reactions. How real was this life she had made? How committed was she to it? Could she give the woman compassion and not get pulled in to the other's world of depression and desire for death? In thinking about these questions the subject tended to see the issue in terms of responsibility. 'I owe a responsibility to myself, but can I deny my responsibility to someone I've called a friend, someone who can turn to no one else for understanding?' Thus she formulated the question as a matter of weight or amount. Which responsibility is the greater? In showing her the power of Death the Tarot shifts the question to a more internal but in fact more practical issue. What can she accomplish? How strong is she? If she chooses her responsibility to her friend can she help, or will she go down herself? And it demands, as well, that she question her motives. How much does death lure her? Will her friend's presence become the means to drop a life that at times is filled with hope, but at other times appears only a pretence, a game?

Before leaving Death we should realize that the usual interpretation works here as well. She had moved to a new place, formed new relationships, started new activities. To the extent that she makes these things real, then the old self, the personality aligned with depression and suicide, has died. The card shows a boat travelling down a shadowy river. Beyond, the sun rises through two stone pillars. To get to her new country she took a boat ride. Do the boats coincide, the physical ferry boat that carried her from one place to another, and the symbolic boat of Death taking the soul from the shadow to the sunrise?

If we place Death and the knight of Pentacles side by side, we notice a strong resemblance.

But where Death's horse slowly prances the knight's stands stolidly on its hilltop. He is not going anywhere. He has his job, his burdens. Pentacles are the suit of work, the material world, practical activities. The knight devotes himself to these mundane things, and the life he symbolizes can seem boring, all responsibility, all work, all external activities. Death carries a banner with a white rose for purity. The knight holds his Pentacle in front of him, conscious of his tasks. Now notice that the points around Death's flower form a pentagram themselves, but a reversed one. Death reverses all values. It turns all accomplishments, all security, upside-down. In the face of death, what does a career mean? Or a home, or even friendship?

If you stand with arms and legs out, your body will form a pentacle. The upright pentacle symbolizes reason and correct behaviour, for the head is above the body. Reversed, the pentacle places the genitals symbol of passion, above the head (see the upside-down pentacle on the Devil). The reversed pentagram in the rose suggests that death is passionate, it overcomes thought, plans, expectations.

Can the knight of Pentacles compete with it? The question is central to this reading. Against the seductive passion of death she has built up a bulwark of rationality. Now, to someone else, these things might seem very real — friendship, art, work, a home. But this woman has seen the emptiness and she has given in, even if partially and in the past, to the absoluteness of death, which overcomes all else. Can anything be real enough to counteract that?

I have posed the question as if the answer was a self-evident no. But in fact it is not clear at all. For in a certain way the knight of Pentacles is exactly what she needs to counter Death. As the suit of Earth, Pentacles represent material reality. They symbolize created things, things you can see and hold and recognize as real. In *Seventy-*

Eight Degrees of Wisdom, Part Two I described the symbolism of linking the four suits of the Tarot to the four letters of God's name. In this system the first three suits, Wands, Cups, and Swords signify the different stages of creation — any form of creation, from God's bringing the world out of nothingness, to an artist painting a portrait, to someone building a house, or making dinner. But the fourth suit, Pentacles, stands for the thing itself — the material world, the picture on the canvas, the house, the food on the table.

The knight of Pentacles symbolizes the practical steps she has taken to build her life. To the extent that she commits herself to that reality, then she commits herself to the idea of a future. She does not counter Death with an emotion, such as confidence, or with philosophy. She counters it with *things*, friendships that become genuine bonds, work she can look at with pride, a house and world to live in. Only — compared to Death, all that can seem so dull, so slow.

And now comes the need to help a friend, someone she has known for longer than she knows anyone in her new home. And of course the knight of Pentacles symbolizes responsibility.

Remember that we used the queen of Pentacles as her significator. That choice, too, helped to emphasize the reality and satisfaction of her new life. The knight endorses the reality of Pentacles, while at the same time indicating a step down from the ideal of the queen. The queen sits solidly in the world, confident of her position. The knight lacks her sense of a secure place. Because the subject gave herself to Death she must re-establish her connections to the living. The knight (as opposed to the page) implies that she has gone some way towards doing this, but in contrast to the third possibility, the king (partner to the queen), it says that her connection is still tentative. She must work to develop it. She must make the effort of pushing through the boring and frustrating problems of housing, jobs, etc. And the card's resemblance to Death provides an eerie reminder that the thirteenth trump still occupies the centre.

In describing the work cycle positions I stressed that the crossing card develops out of the first, rather than opposing it. The encounter with death in the form of her own self-destructive act (and the other's obsession with suicide) pushed her to turn very deliberately toward life (and slow deliberation to the point of boredom is a hallmark of the knight of Pentacles). She moved to a new land, started new activities. But at the same time Death inhabits the knight of Pentacles like a ghost.

When we laid down a line of cards they came out as follows:

Both the cards in the 'preparation' reflect the knight of Pentacles, the seven as a card in the same suit, and the knight of Cups as the other 'yin' knight, and one even closer in image to Death.

Right-side up, the seven of Pentacles indicates that a person has created something substantial in his life. He has worked hard, and now can stop and look with pride and satisfaction at what he has done. As with the nine, the pentacles growing on the bushes symbolize something established which continues to develop and grow. The figure does not put down his tools. The gardener must continue to tend his crops. But his hard effort has brought him to the point where the bush has taken root. It has flowered and he can look at it and think, 'This is real and I have brought it into creation.'

Here, however, the card appears reversed. All these things have not yet happened. She has not lived long enough in her new home, has not found the right work, not shared enough experience with her friends. She remains at the level of the knight, where her efforts seem unrooted, producing only boredom. In the position of past experience the seven of Pentacles reversed tells her that she has not created a strong enough basis to root her during the crisis generated by her friend's request to visit her. She must recognize this weakness and consider it in deciding what to do.

Of all the Minor cards, the knight of Cups most resembles Death. The horses take much the same stance, rivers flow through both cards, the knight holds his cup like Death his banner (though in opposite hands). The resemblance — in the position of expectations — makes the subject conscious of how much death still fills her mind, how much her friend's request becomes an attraction, in the (acceptable) form of an obligation. For the knight of Pentacles Death lurked in the background as a half-forgotten shadow. Here it steps forward, in its slow majesty, to remind her of its dreamlike power. Remember that the knight of Cups is essentially passive. She believes partly in her own passivity in the face of death, but also in facing life. In life we must struggle and work hard to make things grow. The seven of Pentacles' restfulness comes after long effort. The knight of Cups attempts to reject this approach. Without the seven of Pentacles' basis the subject has not decided whether or not she wants to involve herself in life. She does not believe entirely that she *can* involve herself. Spending a period of time outside the realm of life (she and her friend lived virtually alone for several months in their death-dominated world) produces a distance from other people, their attitudes and assumptions. Among its other interpretations, the knight of Cups means isolation.

In recent years a number of psychologists and writers have pointed out that modern society attempts to banish death. We do not talk or think about it, when people suffer terminal diseases everyone tells them, 'Of course you'll get better. You'll live forever,' and when people do die they often do so in hospitals away from family or friends, and then the undertakers embalm the body and make up the face to resemble someone alive. As one result of all this, someone who takes on death's concerns also takes a step outside society. Other people will not understand, will not want to understand. She cannot talk to them about her friend's desire or her own feelings about death. And so the isolation increases. And when she decides to return she may find the path blocked by her own heightened perceptions. People may appear shallow and their interests trivial. Death continues to hold her by the very reality which everyone tries to deny.

If the knight of Cups functions here as Death's stand-in we should not ignore its own meanings. Previous readings have shown us the knight's combination of withdrawal and responsibility. A great part of her wants her friend to leave her alone, and yet she cannot just dismiss the call for help. As an expectation the card says that she views the problem as a classic knight of Cups dilemma. She desires non-involvement, self absorption. But she cannot dismiss the knight's call to duty.

But is this the only way to view the situation? She sees it this way, but can the Tarot suggest another approach? By casting any refusal to help as a rejection of obligation she depicts putting herself first as a kind of passivity. Choosing herself means doing nothing, or not doing what she should be doing. In a way she links herself to Death in either direction. If she 'does the right thing' and agrees to have her friend join her, she once again enters the other's obsession with death. But if she refuses she does so passively, a frame of mind proper to facing death and not life. The three work cards, all solar, open the way for the first time in this reading to life as a real choice and not simply a denial of death.

As the 'youngest' cards the pages stand for beginnings. As the suit of Fire, Wands also represent beginnings. The page of Wands, therefore, symbolizes the beginning of things, but also the attitude suitable for beginnings. He is eager, committed, he declares himself to the world, to himself. 'This is what I want, this is what I will do.' By taking such a firm stand, the page turns the knight's inexperience into a virtue. In contrast to the seven pentacles on the bush, the page stands in a desert. For the beginning element is a long way from the established reality of Earth. And yet, that doesn't matter. If nothing grows now, it will. He will make it grow.

As a card of her 'work' the page tells her she must make a real choice for life. Only in that framework can she decide how to handle her friend's needs. The page says she must not see her activity only as mundane movement to counter Death's absoluteness, but as a real beginning. She needs to allow life to become real to her. And she must recognize that she has indeed dropped to the level of a page. She is starting over, not just trying to return to whatever she had before her involvement with Death. She has come to a new land with new people. By declaring herself a new person she acknowledges how much Death has wiped out her past life and achievements. But declaring herself new also means she can go beyond Death to the new life implied in the card.

The five of Wands shows her involved in that new life. It tells her she needs to overcome the passivity shown in the two reluctant knights. She needs to recognize that life is a struggle, but one she can choose to find exhilarating and not just exhausting. The picture shows five boys in a mock battle. They bang their sticks but do not actually hit each other. If someone withdraws for a time from the competitive mantle of society, then the 'rat-race' may become her sole image of daily life. The five of Wands as a work card tells her she can view such problems as work or housing or ambition as challenges. Some decks based on the Rider pack transform the clash of sticks into a kind of barn-raising, in which the boys are building a wall. In that constructive sense (implied in this picture and especially in this reading) the card becomes a transition between the page of Wands and the seven of Pentacles.

Both the page and the five feature youth as a metaphor for eagerness and beginnings. But youth also implies lack of experience. Strength between the two gives a necessary underpinning of maturity. The card tells her directly that she does have the strength to handle this crisis and she must look for strength within herself, rather than seek support from other people. The image took on an added poignancy when she told me that her friend described her depression as a lion threatening to devour her. In this reading the subject learns that she too must face the lion of her fears, her despair and death urges. Remember that even though Strength is solar its female imagery directs her to find her bearings within. At the same time the two cards around it emphasize Strength's optimism. They tell her not to direct her attention only at her emotions and her past experiences, but to look outward.

Much of what we said about Strength in the previous reading applies here as well. She does not overcome her fear/attraction to death by pushing it away from her, but by allowing it to emerge within a context of her commitment to life. One serious question arises from this card. Where does she direct her strength? Because the lion symbolizes her friend's troubles does it mean she contains the strength to help her friend without becoming swept up as she did before? Or do the surrounding cards of beginnings imply that she must find the strength to say no? The following two cards give a hint of an answer, but because the subject found that answer equivocal she asked to lay out another line.

First, the last two cards. The 'outcome' shows what happens as a result of the different influences. Here we see the seven of Wands reversed. Right-side up the picture shows someone standing on a hill-top beating back an attack. It represents holding yourself together by pushing away your problems. Reversed, the problems overwhelm. He can no longer keep them back. Now, this seemed a fairly ominous suggestion for a reading with such positive work cards, especially when it stayed in the same suit as two of those cards. It implied that the qualities shown in the three cards were not powerful enough to counteract the weaknesses. The seven indicates that she can keep her fears, her depressions — and her friend's problems — at bay for a time, but eventually the Wands approach will give way. Optimism, projects, her new life in general will fail, and all the old things will sweep over her. As a seven it refers to the reversed seven of Pentacles. That card said she lacked a solid base on which to build a life. Here we find that what seemed real and important about her current activities will prove too weak, without basis, and she will give way to her old troubles.

And yet, the work cards seemed to imply something very real. They did not actually recommend the seven of Wands' attitude of pushing everything away. Instead Strength tells her to allow the problems to emerge, but in a context of putting them behind her for a new beginning. What goes wrong? Does the outcome tell her that she will not follow the work recommendations but only pretend to herself that she follows them?

Perhaps the card shows her something else. Perhaps it demonstrates to her the limits of her ability to handle everything, especially the reading's original question, her friend's request. If she tries to keep on top of all her problems she will fall into the middle of them. The work cards tell her she must find strength within herself. The outcome insists she must respect her weakness as well.

And she can use weakness. For the last card in the line, the 'result', does not indicate catastrophe from her failure to triumph over her difficulties. Instead, the ace of Pentacles shows security and the beginnings of the kind of solidity denied to her in both the knight and the seven of Pentacles. Traditionally this ace of Earth signifies wealth and material success. In many readings, however, I have found that it very often stresses a safe environment, one that feels enclosed and protected from outside troubles. We see the usual hand from a cloud holding out the gift of a Pentacle, symbol of the magic found within the material world. The hand appears within a garden surrounded by a wall of flowers. In a number of cards (see the two of Wands below) a garden or enclosed building will represent security. If a garden then this security nurtures the person, but if a wall then the person finds her or himself bound by it and needs to leave or break free.

A path leads to the garden gate, formed by a wreath of leaves and flowers. The gate's oval shape recalls the wreath of victory surrounding the World dancer on the twenty-first trump. Beyond the gate we see mountains, symbols of truth and spiritual development. Therefore, the garden does not stifle, but gives her a place to ground herself in simplicity and material comfort before venturing out again on a path of exploration.

In the work cycle pattern this card comes directly out of the fall shown in the reversed seven of Pentacles. There she discovers her limitations. The shock of that discovery makes her see that she needs to withdraw into some safe surrounding in order to build up her base in the world. This is the 'hint' mentioned above. The work cycle, like all Tarot spreads, does not make her decision for her, but only shows her what she can work with. She must interpret and decide for herself. These cards, however, seem to imply that allowing her friend to visit would provoke a collapse followed by a retreat. Still, because of the uncertainty in meaning, we laid out another line. The cards came out as shown opposite.

We see several of our old friends, beginning with the Hermit. As in the last reading he implies a withdrawal from others for the sake of attending to herself. As past experience, it contains a double meaning. It applies to the time spent in isolation from other people while she tried to take care of her friend. The two of them led a hermit like existence for several months. In fact, of course, the subject did not truly withdraw because she placed herself in another person's service, doing this to such an extent that she allowed the other person's psychic state to engulf her (though she did so partly because of attitudes within herself). For the subject, the true Hermit decision came when

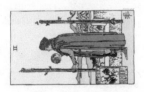

she returned to society, because to do so meant leaving the other person who had dominated her. By 'returning' to a different place she also left behind the environment that now bore associations of despair and suicide.

There is another side to the Hermit in this reading. Her involvement with death separated her from ordinary people, who do their best never to think of such things. Above we observed how difficult a person can find it to return to the outside world with all its illusions and unacknowledged fears. The Hermit picks up on this reluctance to leave the realm of Death.

We see a similar ambivalence in the next card as well. The two of Wands, as we know from an earlier reading, represents success, but success seen as confinement. Unlike the garden of the ace of Pentacles the castle here encloses the man. It belongs to him but he belongs to it. His responsibilities mean he cannot just leave to go out into the world, to explore, or to enjoy the beautiful countryside outside the walls. In the position of expectations the card says a great deal about the subject's ambivalence towards her new life, and especially her commitment to work and ambition. In the line above we saw the Wands' eagerness to throw oneself into activities. Here we see the other side of that desire — the fear of getting trapped.

When the subject came to her new country she also began to work in such areas as the arts and Eastern medicine. She became involved with other people doing these things. Inevitably this raised the question of ambition. While she wanted very much to develop her skills and to express herself, the idea of success appeared to her as it does to many people — tainted. It seemed to go against ideals of 'purity'. Moreover a side of her wanted to travel, to live as freely as possible. As much as she desired accomplishment, therefore, a part of her believed that success brings confinement and not satisfaction.

If we go back to her original question we can see another ambivalence in the card. The figure stands alone in her castle, cut off from other people as well as her own freedom. The image expresses her sense of guilt at the thought of refusing her friend's request. However much she thinks she should put herself first, she also thinks, 'This woman has no one else. What right do I have to reject her? Can I set myself up as some sort of lord of the manor, telling her she can't come in? And for what? Material comfort? Success?

And yet, she knows — from the reversed seven of Pentacles, from her own disastrous past attempts — that she cannot singlehandedly save this woman from despair. Whether or not any outside agencies could accomplish such a rescue is not the issue. She cannot. In the middle of her three work cards the Empress reversed tells her she must look at the situation with a clear mind. Right-side up, the card signifies passion; upside-down, it calls for a rejection of passion in favour of reason. The card tells her to reject emotional responses, reject the image of herself as mothering the other woman, and to decide what to do on the basis of a careful consideration of possibilities.

Mythologically the Empress symbolizes the Great Mother, who rules the world with love. Psychologically she symbolizes the passionate approach to life, acting and reacting from feelings. Reversed it tells her to turn away from those responses. She cannot function as her friend's all-protective mother, she cannot fill the world with a mother's love.

The reversed Empress does not signify only a rejection of emotion. It shows an awakening of that which lies dormant under the rule of emotion — analysis, rational weighing of the various elements, as well as outside requirements. The card comes under Strength in the line above it. By advising her to limit her emotions, the Empress also implies a restriction to Strength. Because her new life (the page and five of Wands) has made her stronger, she must not assume she can handle all situations. Some lions she cannot tame so easily.

On the sides of the Empress we find the eight of Wands reversed, and the three of Pentacles reversed. We have seen both these cards before in this book, and we know that in their different ways they both signify frustration. In the first line the work cards around Strength symbolized positive attitudes to take as part of her development. In this line the cards show problems she must recognize in order to accept or overcome them. When difficulties appear in the work cards they tell us first of all to become aware of them and then to look for the best approach.

The eight of Wands reversed tells her that the tensions in her life will not go away quickly. She cannot expect an easy resolution to her difficulties. Nor will the rash start shown above bring quick results. A long process lies ahead of her before she can reach the seven of Pentacles state of looking back with satisfaction at the life she has built for herself.

The reversed three of Pentacles means mediocre work or a lack of development to a level of mastery. Both elements come into play here. 'Mediocrity' is something she must avoid. The card acts as a warning against sloppy or half-hearted work. As a lack of development the card reminds her that she must accept this limitation in order to eventually go beyond it. She is not yet a master at her different skills. Pretending to herself that she is will lead to mediocrity.

The subject was a woman of many talents and interests. In the past she had studied and worked at various vocations without completely satisfying herself that she had fulfilled her potential in any of these areas. (This history recalls the first Celtic cross reading, where the three of Pentacles reversed carried much the same meaning.) And then came the period ruled by Death, when all effort became overshadowed. The subject told me how she and her friend first came together through shared artistic interests. Her friend had gone further than she had and the subject thought she could learn and advance. But then despair took over and all these activities ended.

Now she wishes to return to meaningful work. But she has lost time, her skills have dulled, and they were skills that had never reached their highest levels in the first place. And so the importance of the eight of Wands reversed comes in to add to the frustration of not fulfilling the potential implied in the three of Pentacles. By warning her of these things the reading helps her to deal with them.

Often in a work cycle the card of expectation will dominate the character of the cards that come after it. We did not see this so much in the first line where the three work cards advised her to leave the knight of Cups' passivity behind. Here, however, the ambivalence we saw in the two of Wands casts its shadow in the three cards coming after it. For if success means isolation and loss of freedom, why should she work hard, or study, or try to reach some vague potential for mastery? What kind of life is it where she must give up her emotions, her compassion for a friend's suffering, in exchange for some cold intellectualism? And behind all these uncertainties lies the lure of Death, absolute, without limitations, demanding no long effort.

The idea that Death remains her centre through the reading does not imply that she wishes to die or that she will commit suicide. Rather, it prevents her from the commitment to life urged in the first line. It makes it that much harder to endure frustration.

In the first line the seven of Wands reversed reflected the dangers of over-optimism. Even though the work cards recommended that she take a Wands approach, the seven reminded her that she had only begun, and must not confuse eagerness with ability and think she can handle all problems. Here in the second line the work cards take a more negative approach. At the same time they express a greater realism, or at least one that acknowledges her weaknesses. As a consequence the outcome card shows a surfacing of some of the more disturbing attitudes and fears. But just as the ace of Pentacles showed a peaceful result from the defeat of the seven of Wands reversed so the result card here indicates a fresh maturity.

Right-side up the page of Cups signifies allowing the contents of the mind to rise up from the hidden waters of the unconscious. He stands at ease, looking on as the fish of imagination pokes its head out of the cup. Reversed, the experience becomes more unsettling. Fears, resentments, negativities, they all emerge from their hiding places. The reversed page of Cups exposes these things. The page of Wands would deny them by claiming to have started all over. The Wands attitude is necessary, valuable. She needs to look towards life, towards beginnings. But she must not deny the past or the way its invisible hands can still drag her backwards. In this card that past rises up, and even though she may find the experience painful or frightening it leads beyond the *page* of Wands to the king.

The page of Cups also reflects the knight of Cups. There we saw a desire to remain withdrawn, looking dreamily into her cup. But the knight does not really consider what he will see in that cup. He simply wants to be left alone. Here the cup brings up the very disturbances we hoped to ignore. The request of her friend to join her is the trigger for this eruption but it spreads beyond that immediate crisis, reaching back to her own relationship with Death, forward to her mixed feelings about work and success.

The surfacing of these things would seem to clear away a good deal of her uncertainties, for the result card, the king of Wands reversed, indicates maturity and toughness. For many of the court cards the reversed side shows a weakening of the image's basic qualities. But Wands, and particularly the king, convey such a one-sided optimism that reversing them can bring in a greater tolerance for human weakness. For someone like the subject, who has breathed in despair and walked with death, the booming optimism of the king right-side up is an impassibility. In a certain way the page of Wands, for all its valuable affirmation, attempts to strike a *pose* of optimism. But the page of Cups reversed does not allow it. By undermining the pose it makes room for a more mature commitment to the basic Wands desire for life.

The reversed king learns compassion, but he learns toughness as well. In describing this card Waite used the formula, 'Good but severe; austere, yet tolerant.' The gentle qualities may show on the outside, but within she becomes not hard, or cruel, but simply firm. Unyielding, not out of selfishness or cruelty, but out of her own desire to live.

Above, we saw that the Tarot does not make your decisions for you. This reading probably comes as close as any to saying, 'Do this and not that.' Several days after the reading I saw the subject again.

She told me that she had written to her friend that she must not come to visit her.

WORK CYCLE TWO

This reading comes from a woman who has done a series of work cycle readings with me. She sees them as a way of keeping check on her development. By noticing how the readings follow each other and how they change, and especially which images recur, she can also use them as aids in that development. As part of the commentary for this reading, therefore, we will look at several cards from the readings before and after it.

Two themes run through most of this woman's readings. First is the question of her work. A successful translator, she had become dissatisfied with this occupation and had decided to invoke her lifelong interest in dance by starting an agency for dancers and related professionals. The second theme is that of her relationships with others, particularly with lovers, and with her mother. Both these concerns appear in this reading, for while she came to ask about her work, shortly before the reading she had broken up with a man with whom she had hoped to build a longtime relationship.

For significator we used the queen of Pentacles, and when she had mixed the cards I laid them out as shown opposite.

The reading begins with two Cups cards, each in its way signifying joy or the lack of it. Right-side up the ten symbolizes family, celebration of happiness and love. She had just lost a chance for this kind of satisfaction in life — or so it had seemed at the time of the breakup. By the time of the reading she had begun to perceive that this particular relationship never really held out a true promise of the ten of Cups. The card did not signify so much a loss as a realization that it was never there.

How far does this lack extend? The reading ends with the ten of Pentacles, which, as we shall see, is a kind of sober cousin to the ten of Cups. Instead of outpourings of happiness it provides security, stability. Therefore, it represents a compromise with the happiness that she cannot find in her environment. And the ten of Pentacles follows Justice, which means that she recognizes certain truths in order to achieve that stability. These truths include the fact that her life in general lacks the base of a supportive family history. When the subject was only an infant her father left his wife and child so that her mother had raised her alone. Despite her mother's love for her she had felt strongly the lack of a father, as well as the pain of desertion.

Also, the forced intimacy of her relationship with her mother meant that she had had to forfeit some of the unthinking security that gives childhood its protected quality.

Though much of this information comes from previous readings, the cover card highlights it. Look at the ten of Cups right-side up.

The two parents celebrate the rainbow. They salute it, which is to say they acknowledge that life has given them this gift of joy. But the children dance along without looking up. The efforts of their parents to shield them from life's troubles give them the privilege of taking happiness for granted. Conscious of her mother's difficulties and need for support the subject lacked exactly this privilege in her life. In her previous reading the six of Cups appeared as the first card.

In this picture we see a child in a garden being given a gift. The picture conveys the idea of protection, but in an intense, almost cloying way.

In that reading we decided together that the card represented a fantasy of childhood that she carried with her even as an adult. In this reading, in the ten of Cups reversed, we see the reality.

In that earlier reading we also looked at the possibility that she had come to occupy the position of the older child and her mother the younger one. In other words, she felt called upon at times to protect and help her mother. Alone, the two of them had only each other, and sometimes (especially now that she had become an adult) the roles would shift back and forth between them. Again, compare this situation to the ten, where the father and mother hold each other, leaving the children free to play.

Now bring this back to the present. For if the lack of security while growing up hurt her that sense of loss or something missing remains, and she seeks it in her relationships with men. She longs for home and family, and for a man who will be a father as well as lover (another meaning of the six of Cups). At this time, however, the reading tells her she will not find these things through others. She must first build a base for herself in her own life (the ten of Pentacles) even if this appears to lack the overflowing joy she desires. Notice that even though the immediate concern is the breakup of a love affair the card describing it is not the Lovers reversed, or the two of Cups reversed, but the ten reversed. The loss, or lack of family, not romance.

At this point we should take a moment to observe something about Tarot readings and personal history. Most people think of readings as a kind of clairvoyance, where the cards stimulate the reader to uncover hidden details about the subject's life. In this model the subject of this reading would have come to me as a stranger and from the cards I would have discovered that her father had abandoned her and her mother, that she and her lover had broken up, and so on. In fact, however, I knew these things because she told me (though some of them had come up in the readings we did). The ten of Cups reversed and the six of Cups did not reveal these facts; they exposed them, lifted them up from the background of her life, so that she could look at them in a new way. By summarizing her past in visual symbols, the cards give her a way to focus her awareness of her own experiences.

Each card in the Tarot deck, each set of symbols, carries specific meanings. As soon as they enter a reading, however, they become unique. They become renewed for that person at the moment. In this kind of reading the task of the reader becomes to open the way into the symbols, to show the person how they apply, to point out the relationships between the images in their different positions, and to help the person use this information in some worthwhile way. If

I did not know anything of the subject's history I would have seen from the cards alone that she lacked an environment of love and family, that she was trying to counter this with pleasure (the nine of Cups — I might have guessed from this crossing card that she had recently suffered some disappointment), that the problem came from some deeper cause (the Magician reversed) and that she needed to look honestly at her life in order to achieve stability (Justice and the ten of Pentacles). However, the fact that I knew certain things beforehand enabled both of us to penetrate more deeply into the symbols.

The nine of Cups crosses the ten of Cups reversed. As mentioned above, the nine also shows joy, but of a more limited sort. This plump figure with his slightly smug smile and his table full of Cups represents physical pleasure — parties, late nights, excitement. Coming out of the disappointment shown in the ten reversed it says that the subject tries to distract herself. In some readings this card would signify just what the person needed. Here, however, the card of Justice as the outcome indicates that other issues are at stake. When reversed the nine of Cups changes its character. Instead of superficiality or escapism it signifies truth, freedom. When we know of this other possibility we can see that upright the card implies a refusal to look at truth — the very quality called for in Justice. And when we realize that the Magician reversed as past experience indicates that something is not right within her, or that the six of Pentacles as a work card tells her that she must open herself to whatever 'aid' she may receive (below we will look at the six of Pentacles as the 'disguised' principle of Justice in daily life), then the nine of Cups takes on more and more of its escapist qualities.

But escape from what? And if the reversed card symbolizes truth and liberation, truth about what? Liberation from what? In the immediate situation it refers to the unhappiness caused by the breakup, and says that she cannot escape this pain. Only through understanding what went wrong, including her own misplaced hopes about the relationship, does she 'liberate' herself from the hurt and loss.

But if the ten of Cups reversed — and the Magician reversed — refer to something deeper than the immediate situation then the nine of Cups also refers to a larger pattern than her immediate disappointment. Her life has included the lack of a full family as a child, and now as an adult she reaches for that kind of life while covering her longing with excitement. 'Truth' means recognizing just how deeply the ten of Cups reversed has hurt her, and 'liberation' means to overcome that loss through acceptance.

A confirmation of this approach came in the following reading we did together. (Obviously we could not draw on such information when we looked at *this* reading. However, these commentaries do not attempt to mimic the conditions at the time of the actual reading but to see into them as deeply as possible. And when we did the following reading we looked back at this one with the information gained from the new set of images.) In that reading the Magician reversed appeared again, but now it had moved from the past to one of the work cards in the present. This change implied that she had brought the problem to consciousness and could work on it. In the position of past experience, vacated by the Magician, we found the nine of Swords. The card of sorrow.

In the current reading the Magician reversed as 'past' makes her aware of some essential block on her realizing her creative power. Something has turned that power upside-down. When she moves that problem out of the realm of 'given' into something she is working on she finds, like something uncovered by rolling away a stone, the hidden anguish of the nine of Swords.

This book takes as one of its working assumptions that cards of the same number will usually relate to each other. The situation 'transmutes' from the one suit to the other, as I have described elsewhere. In our primary reading we see the escapist nine of Cups, implying that she avoids the truth about something, and so cannot free herself from it. In the following, the nine of Swords appears as past experience. The card does not tell her specifically what sorrow it represents. Only she can discover that, by following Justice into her past. The card does make it clear that what blocks her, what makes her seek excitement, is the distress of old and hidden pain.

Returning to our basic reading we come to the reversed Magician as past experience. Right-side up the card signifies the solar or creative principle. The Magician acts, he brings forth life. He does so not through personal will or control, but by making himself an open channel for spiritual energy. Many creative people — artists, scientists, teachers — have said how they experience their power as a kind of impersonal stream which passes through the filter of their minds and experiences to emerge as ideas and concrete works. And so we see the Magician's famous gesture: the Wand raised like a lightning rod to heaven, the finger grounding the current in the material world.

Now, the subject too had experienced herself as a channel for creative power, especially when she began her agency. And yet, at each time, when she thought she established herself, something would happen. The opportunities would dwindle. Projects would fall through. And she would become sick. Drawn-out illness would debilitate her, making it impossible to push forward.

To some extent her weak constitution was simply a limitation she needed to accept. Referring again to that following reading it contained three Wands cards, the two as the cover card, the ace crossing it, and the ten as result.

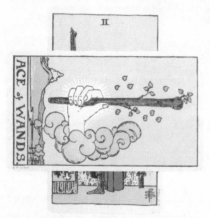

The two indicated that her work had developed to a more stable situation. Out of that came the ace, signifying a great release of energy as a result of the hard work done to create a foundation (the two readings took place six months apart). But the final card, the ten, was the card of burdens. In discussing this progression she said it represented her tendency to get excited and take on too many projects which then would wear her down. As a result of that reading she decided to look carefully at proposals and limit her plans by her capacity as well as by her interest.

So her tendency towards illness came partly from physical limitations. Yet weakness, especially at the exact time when a person needs strength, brings us back to the reversed Magician. We experience it as instability, inadequacy, depression. The subject often found that in her ace of Wands bursts of enthusiasm she would feel strong, confident, tremendously excited. And then, if things didn't work out, there would come a crash, almost as if the Magician would work right-side up for a while, and then flip over, leaving her drained and helpless, until such time as she could gather her energy. In fact, the excited part of the cycle also belongs to the reversed Magician. With the channel for psychic energy blocked she builds up a charge during those depressed weak periods. Thus she emerges with a bang — enthusiasm, projects, confidence. Her work goes well, she draws people and opportunities to herself. But unless she can open the channels so the energy will replenish itself she eventually runs the charge down. The plans fail to develop, or a relationship collapses, she becomes ill and withdraws into herself to give the charge time to build again.

The four of Swords reversed as the expectation signifies her determination to bring herself out of this cycle. She rightly sees the key to release not in the periods of excitement, but in those of depression. Right-side up the four of Swords depicts her previous habit whenever her body would give way or her world would fall around her. She would go into hiding, not seeing her friends, cutting back her work as much as possible. The picture shows a knight lying in a deathlike pose in a dim church. He brings to mind various figures of myth and folktales who lie in a trance after suffering spiritual wounds — the Fisher King in the Grail legends, Sleeping Beauty. But here the card is reversed. Unlike Sleeping Beauty, the subject will no longer wait for some outside rescuer to break through the barrier and wake her with his magic force. She recognizes that she must become her own Magician. She must not allow herself to keep withdrawing into the enchanted castle of her lethargy.

In her previous reading the four of Swords, right-side up, occupied the centre of a line that began with the Hermit and the Moon. Its position as the central card indicated the force of that habit of withdrawal. Through that reading and through her general attempts to understand herself, she became more conscious of this pattern of behaviour. Her desire to change it, her belief that she can change it, shows up in the current reading by the four of Swords reversing itself and moving from work to expectations.

In the past, during her enthusiastic periods, she would tell herself,

'I'm going to be careful this time, take care of myself, not get too wound up. I won't let myself collapse.' Now she perceives the value of starting from the bottom. She will refuse to give in at the point of greatest vulnerability. This decision helps open the way for Justice. With its implications of honesty and determination the four of Swords reversed implies an alternative to the escapism of the nine of Cups.

Traditionally, the four of Swords symbolizes caution as well as the refusal to hide. She knows that she cannot burst loose from the castle, for then the cycle will repeat itself. If she wishes to end the pattern she will have to do so carefully. She must not hide, from others or from herself, and this includes allowing her weakness to emerge as something she can use to understand her life.

The work cards shift attention away from the emotional issues to her original question, that of advice about her work. The eight of Pentacles reversed reminds her that she must develop her skills and learn the ways of her new profession. Right-side up the card shows an apprentice learning his craft. He does not attempt to set himself up as a master or to sell his pentacles, he continues to develop his technique. Upside-down it can signify impatience, or the desire to rush ahead without building a base. As a work card it tells her to avoid the illusion of large projects until she knows her way in the field. In discussing this card she told me how great plans sometimes marked her excited periods. The lack of groundwork for these plans led to their failure to materialize, and this in turn brought on depression.

The second card, also an eight, picks up on this idea. It tells her to look for activities that will produce definite results. She needs this kind of fulfilment for her agency to build up a reputation, and for her own satisfaction at seeing some of the arrows come to earth.

In the first Celtic cross reading in this book we saw that the reversed eight of Wands referred to 'arrows of jealousy'. The meaning came from the right-side up interpretation of 'arrows of love'. Usually an image of romance, the arrows here refer to one of her underlying concerns in this reading, how to handle her relationship with her mother. The card tells her to direct love at her mother and to avoid situations producing jealousy. That emotion would sometimes arise in the intense six of Wands atmosphere. It became a particular problem during the subject's periods of excitement when she often felt her mother jealous of her activities. The eight of Wands tells her she can counteract jealousy with love.

The six of Pentacles is a complex card, with certain 'hidden' meanings that do not always rise to the surface in a reading. Since these meanings connect the card to Justice, and Justice appears beside it, we can assume that the card's esoteric quality does emerge here. More important, the four of Swords reversed had shown a determination to break out of the cycle. That decision implies an openness to the particular elements symbolized in the six of Pentacles.

Among its ordinary meanings the six of Pentacles can refer to a particular kind of relationship, one in which the people do not find themselves at ease or do not deal with each other according to their feelings, but according to rules or hierarchies. Sometimes one takes the superior position, so that the other (or others) must approach like a beggar pleading for attention or acceptance. At other times neither person feels in control; the past keeps them both on their knees, and the stiffness between them measures out how much love and openness they can share with each other. Both conditions describe aspects of the problem between the subject and her mother.

In the previous reading the six of Cups as the cover card depicted the subject's longing as a child for that feeling of protection. But she also saw that it showed a role-reversal between herself and her mother, for now that she had grown up and achieved some success the subject found that her mother would sometimes use weakness as a way of pushing her daughter to do things for her, a way of keeping her close. Now, in this reading, another six, Pentacles, continues this idea. Her mother's pose puts the subject in the position of the merchant, but in fact the tension makes both of them beggars to the situation. As a work card it tells her she needs to change this pattern (perhaps by refusing to participate on such terms) if she wishes to go beyond the ten of Cups reversed.

In regard to her career the six of Pentacles suggests the possibility of receiving aid from someone more established than herself. Because the merchant measures out his contribution she cannot expect some lavish gift but rather something that can help her along the way. As a work card, it offers her opportunity while reminding her to rely on her own efforts. (Some time after this reading the subject encountered the European representative of a major American performer. While he told her he could not guarantee the organization would support her projects he did say that if she put together a good proposal he would do what he could to help her get backing.)

If we turn the imagery around and see the subject as the merchant then the card tells her to limit her time and energy, especially what she gives to other people. By doing this she first of all takes practical steps in regard to her physical problems. Instead of trying to pretend she can do everything she learns to act within her limitations. These steps can benefit her emotionally as well. Like many people the subject found it difficult to refuse anyone's call for help or attention. The importance of the ten of Wands in her readings refers not just to taking on too many projects but also to accepting other people's burdens. And because she would extend herself so much for others, when the collapse came, she would swing the other way and isolate herself, as in the four of Swords. If she wishes to end that tendency to withdrawal she must first end the habit of holding nothing back from her friends (and her mother). The six of Pentacles advises her to give to others what she can afford.

The idea that she isolates herself in times of trouble swings the image round again, putting her back in the position of the beggars and suggesting to her that she learn to ask for help when she needs it. By its harshness the image of a beggar challenges her. She would rather envisage help as the six of Cups, where the little girl does not need to ask for anything, but simply stands there receiving love and protection. But the six of Pentacles as a work card makes her see the unreality of that image. To get aid we must learn to ask, exposing our weaknesses, saying, 'Look at me, I'm hurt, I'm in trouble. Will you help me?'

The image of the beggar brings us to the hidden meanings of the card. In *Seventy-Eight Degrees of Wisdom, Part Two* I described in detail the experiences and thoughts that led me to see this card as a symbol for the principle of Justice at work in the world. A pictorial clue to this concept came from the scales the figure holds. Balanced like those on the trump they imply that events happen according to unknown factors of cause and effect. A verbal clue came from Waite's description of the man as 'in the guise of a merchant'. I cannot say what Waite intended by this expression, but this term 'guise', so close to 'disguise', can imply that Justice (or karma, or psychic laws) acts in the world through the agencies of everyday life.

The beggars hold out their hands and the man gives them coins. The imagery suggests that we can approach Justice as a beneficent force and receive assistance in our difficulties. But we must do so with humility, not demanding that life reward us for our virtues or our efforts, but only open ourselves to the possibility of help. If we take the attitude that ego and determination can solve all problems, then we close ourselves to aid. The Christian tradition of praying on the knees with clasped hands comes from the understanding that we need to shake ourselves loose from the narrow pride that recognizes no power in life beyond individual effort.

The approach to Justice takes the form of what I call 'putting yourself in a position to receive.' This means first of all dedicating yourself to some serious activity. Many people who involve themselves in spiritual development or creative work have commented on the way 'coincidences' occur to smooth them over blocks that may develop along the way. A friend of mine once told me that he needed to consult a certain out of print book. After trying libraries and second-hand bookshops he had run out of places to look when someone he hadn't seen in months came by to visit — carrying a copy of the book.

Almost anyone who dedicates her or himself to some worthwhile activity can tell similar stories of the help they've received at different moments. Usually it will not take the form of a dramatic change or breakthrough, but only a boost over some particular obstacle. Only a few coins measured out by the merchant.

Putting yourself in a position to receive can also mean making some extra effort without any expectation of reward. In *Seventy-Eight Degrees of Wisdom, Part Two* I described how at a crucial time in my life I accompanied my father to the synagogue on a Saturday morning, something I rarely did. In the commentary on that day's Torah reading I found a note that first of all answered a question I'd had in my mind, and much more important, answered it in such a way that it helped me through the crisis I was facing. Now, my own effort took several forms. First of all, the question in my mind exposed me to spirituality (even though the interest came out of intellectual curiousity), for it concerned the translation of one of God's names, 'Shaddai'. Secondly, I went along with my father, literally putting myself in a place to receive. And once there, I made the effort of reading the book. None of these things came from any expectation of aid, even though I should mention that several days earlier I'd done a reading which contained the six of Pentacles. I'd interpreted that card as the possibility of help, but there was no way to predict how that help would come.

Which brings us to the final aspect of receiving — that of paying attention. Because this help does not come as obvious change, because we must open ourselves to these small boosts, we must notice what happens in our lives and pay attention to the significance of small events. Disguised Justice measures out its effects partly because we could not absorb sudden or total change. And partly so we will learn to ask, and partly so we will struggle with the gift and so make proper use of it.

When we apply all these ideas to the subject we see that the card advises her to work steadily towards her goals (this in connection with the warning shown in the eight of Pentacles reversed) while making extra efforts or going places that might make possible unexpected assistance. It advises her to make herself aware of her own actions and emotions. As a work card, it calls for humility, towards others and towards her own limited understanding. For paying attention means to look for the meaning in events, but not as the proud ego deciphering the world. Rather, it tells her to take the position of the beggar, recognizing her weakness and looking for whatever help life will give her.

Justice as the outcome indicates that the hidden principle becomes more evident. Through humility and paying attention she makes herself more conscious of the sources of the current situation. Justice looks to causes and origins. We have seen in previous readings how the imagery of Justice implies the Magician (as well as the High Priestess). The line begins with the Magician reversed as a weakness in her life. At the end, with Justice right-side up, she begins to perceive some of the factors behind that weakness. The discovery, in her next reading, of the nine of Swords 'underneath' the Magician is part of Justice as the outcome in this reading.

When we discussed Justice the subject commented that she had rarely received it in her readings despite the fact that she was someone who sought understanding and enlightenment. In a way, the reading implies that she sought it too hard, trying to push Justice to appear. The six of Pentacles says that she can allow it to happen.

Justice means changes in her life. 'Just' changes. By attending to her own work (both spiritual and practical) and by asking for help without demanding anything, she allows things to work out the way they 'should'. The Tarot contains certain biases about the world. It assumes, for instance, the existence of an unconscious of formless energy and a superconscious of transformed awareness. It also assumes that (sometimes at least) people will get from life what they deserve. The reading tells her that if she does what she needs to do — pursue her work, limit the way she extends herself to others, learn her weaknesses and their causes — her life will lift out of the damaging cycle of enthusiasm/collapse. She will receive Justice.

The reading does not predict the specific changes that will occur but it does say something about the character of these changes. The ten of Pentacles symbolizes stability and an environment that provides support and security at the expense of excitement. Therefore, she should not expect that Justice will mean great changes or revelations, but rather the emergence of stability.

The reading began with the ten of Cups reversed, showing that she longed for a joyous environment, filled with love and celebration. In contrast to the dancing children and the thrilled couple of the Cups card the ten of Pentacles shows a family who look almost bored. Magic fills the card. The ten Pentacles form an image of the Kabbalist tree of life; an old man in a coat of many colours sits outside the gate like some mythical visitor; and a magic wand rests against the archway. None of the three people inside notices these things. Instead, they give an impression of impatience or dissatisfaction. Reversed, the card often means taking risks, so that right-side up it can mean safety and a feeling of annoyance at staying home instead of venturing into the unknown.

In some contexts the card can admonish the person to look beyond security for love, or adventure. In this reading, however, the ten of Pentacles is just what the woman needs. Rather than longing for something she cannot have at this time (the ten of Cups) she must find stability. And she must recognize and embrace the magic in a stable life. The desire for outpourings of joy has led her to extend herself beyond her limits until she collapses. The combination of Justice and the ten of Pentacles releases her from the cycle. With a real base in the present she can begin to free herself from the regrets of the past.

WORK CYCLE THREE

Many people assume a Tarot reading must ask a specific question, or at least address a particular issue. We have seen this sort of reading in this book with the man concerned about the magazine article or the woman whose depressed friend wanted to visit her. People have come to me with very definite questions. 'Will I get the job?' 'Can I succeed as an artist?' Depending on the precision of the question the Tarot will give more or less specific answers.

In one reading a man asked whether a business deal would come through in the following week. I told him the cards indicated a delay but the deal would succeed. This was impossible, he told me, the answer must come in the next few days. Several weeks later I happened to meet him on the street. To his great surprise the other person had put off any decision for two weeks and then finally agreed to go ahead.

Such rare exercises in predictive divination come from the kind of question. More often people will ask for understanding about some crisis (most often romantic). Then the cards will avoid giving direct instructions, though they may make it clear that one choice or another will lead to constructive or destructive results.

If this book has emphasized people with particular concerns there are also many occasions when people will want their cards read as a check on the issues and influences currently at work in their lives.

The following reading, like the previous one, came from a woman who has used the cards often as a guide to understanding the direction and progress of her life. A poet as well as a student of healing and psychic development she was used to visualizing her current moment of development in terms of the Tarot's symbolic system. This will become especially apparent when we look at the meditation done with the cards after the reading. Though she sought real changes in her life she experienced the meditation as a play within the images.

The meditation holds a special interest for us, since the reading, and therefore the mandala pattern, contains the same configuration of the knight of Cups leading to the queen of Cups reversed as the reading we saw in the previous section. There the knight of Cups was the outcome and the queen the possible outcome. Here the knight is again the outcome, with the queen reversed as the result. The problem is virtually the same, but we will see that the two people approach it in their meditations in different ways.

For significator we used the knight of Wands. When we laid the cards they came out as shown opposite.

The image of water carries through much of this reading. We see it in the two Cups cards at the end, but also in several cards belonging to the other elements. The two trumps contain water, as do the six of Swords and the three of Wands. Water symbolizes the flow of life, its adaptability and movement. It symbolizes as well her access to her own feelings.

In the Emperor that access is severely limited. The river of passion found in trump three, the Empress, narrows down to a trickle in the fourth trump. We see it behind the throne, slowly cutting its way through the rock of rules and habit and fixed ideas. In most Tarot decks the Emperor appears somewhat differently. Still a bearded man, he sits with his profile to us, one leg crossing the other to form the number four (compare the Hanged Man and the World). In these decks he signifies the laws and structures of the universe, embodied in the representation of God titled 'the ancient of days'. We can only see him from the side because we cannot know God or even God's law directly.

The Rider pack's Emperor faces us directly. He represents the narrower concept of society. Social structure. The rules of civilization. The Empress comes first in the Major Arcana because nature exists before human law. The Emperor is necessary, for without imposing some sort of form on nature and our own desires human beings would not last very long in the world. Civilization allows us to transmit wisdom, technology, and morality from one generation to the next.

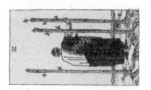

It creates opportunities for people (at least some people) to do something more with their lives than scramble for food and shelter.

And yet, civilization clamps down on the Empress's natural impulses and channels them through a code of morality. It takes the lush garden and turns it to stone. Ideally we should absorb the teachings and codes of our society into ourselves through our parents and our schooling, so that they become natural and easy for us. In that way they would provide a structure through which we could understand the world and act in it. The Emperor would represent opportunity rather than restriction.

In practice, however, many people experience society and its rules as oppressive. Some battle against it, through rebellion of one kind or another. Others take in the commands and opinions of the outside to a level where they cannot move freely, yet cannot just put the rules aside and go their own way. They feel a pressure from a society that basically remains alien to them. The Emperor becomes a force they cannot escape, a force without benefit as it narrows the river of their lives to a stream pushing its way through rock.

The subject was a woman who tried very much to live her own life, ignoring the expectations of the society around her. And yet, she often felt a pressure on her — and within her — making it difficult to freely pursue her interests. Sometimes she identified this pressure as the way the outside world would look at her, at other times she just felt a great guilt. She could not accept the Emperor, but she could not ignore him either.

In discussing this card the subject told me how the night before the reading she had dreamed of burying her parents in her lover's pillowcase. Now, sexual desire belongs to the Empress. Like the river it flows out of nowhere to burst into our lives. But the Emperor demands that sexual practices and even desire follow his strict moral codes. Some people take on these codes as their own, others rebel against them, while still others ignore them — or try to. The subject did as she wanted, but she could not relax about it. The Emperor remained over her.

The dream about her parents suggests a more specific meaning for the Emperor. Her father. A number of times in readings the fourth trump has signified the dominant presence of the father in the person's life. This meaning does not conflict with the Emperor as society. In the traditional family structure the mother provides love and the father authority. We come from our mothers' bodies, our mothers feed us and clean us. But our fathers keep a certain distance. They come forward with love, but often not in the intimate way of our mothers, who have known our bodies as part of their own. And the traditional role of father calls for him to instruct and discipline.

The subject described her father as someone whom she loved and who loved her very deeply, yet who dominated his family — not in a harsh way, but all the more powerfully because of mixing his dominance with love. We should stress that this belief did not come from her father threatening her, but rather from his attitudes taken inside herself. Archetypes will often distort reality by strengthening one aspect of it, and it is not so much her father as an actual person, but the archetype of the Emperor/father working on her in this reading.

The discussion of the Emperor as repression should not take us away from the deeper meanings of the trump. In *Seventy-Eight Degrees of Wisdom, Part Two* I described a meditation fantasy I did with a student of mine who found the Emperor alien and stifling. In her fantasy she came to a barren plain where people sat hunched over workbenches producing objects for a harsh figure on a throne. All the workers wore hoods preventing them from looking up. She found herself frightened to approach the Emperor but managed to push herself forward. As she came closer and forced herself to lift her head she found that she could glimpse something beyond the Emperor. A vast figure, half seen, filled the sky, radiating calm and benevolence. Stars appeared within his body. Against that background the man on the throne dwindled to a puppet. He did not disappear but he no longer terrified. She had come to realize that something much larger existed in the idea of structure.

For the universe takes form as structure, it functions according to laws, some known, some concealed. In recent years cosmologists have considered all the various factors that go into making the universe hospitable to life. There are so many factors, and some in such a narrow range of usefulness (temperature, atmosphere density, the 'correct' strength of gravity to keep planets in the 'correct' orbit and so on) that many scientists have found they cannot escape the conclusion of consciousness taking a part in the shaping of the universe.

The Emperor can represent these greater laws and forms, including the psychic and spiritual as well as the physical. Pondering the trump can lead to an awareness of such laws and the ability to move within them. But as long as we see only social rules — and experience those rules as repressive — then the wider meaning of structures remains blocked from us. The task of this reading becomes partly to get past repression into an appreciation of the inner laws which make life possible.

The six of Swords crosses the Emperor. A card of eerie calm, it conveys a sad and silent quality. The huddled figures, the ferryman with his black pole, the twilight and the dim land all suggest the journey of the dead souls across the river Styx. With the rigidity of the Emperor within her, she finds in her outer life that she cannot act freely, cannot do what she pleases without guilt. She cannot *speak*, and by speech I do not mean only verbal communication. Speech can also mean turning your being in the world into a statement.

The water represents the emotional life. Except for right around the boat the water remains calm. In the immediate events of her life, she can create a stir, make her passage known, but in the wider circles of her past and her sense of the future, the water remains a placid surface disguising the depths beneath it. We see this as well in the three of Wands where she will send her boats but doesn't dare to enter the water herself. In the work cards the Star tells her not to fear disturbing the water.

In water all forms dissolve. If the Emperor symbolizes rigidity then he must dam the river until it becomes only a trickle, allowing life to continue but not to run free. Here she moves upon the water but will not allow herself to excite it. The swords signify sorrows and burdens. She carries them with her and they do not trouble her because they are not conscious. They are simply the boat's cargo, her life's cargo. But what if she tries to remove them — bring to the surface the pains and repressions of the past? She does not dare, for she fears that if she removes the swords the holes will open up and the boat will sink into the water. She will drown in emotion and memory. And so she accepts the twilight and the silence.

In general the six of Swords symbolizes emotional silence. Specifically it represents sexual difficulties and blocks in her relationship with her lover. Her parents disapproved of this relationship. Even though she consciously rejected their views she found it difficult to escape the guilt of disobeying the Emperor. Her dream of burying her parents in her lover's pillowcase came out of that guilt. The difficulty in expressing herself sexually forms another kind of silence.

But the card implies a great power as well. For within silence lies the possibility of speech. And when the huddled figure, the dead soul, throws off her shroud, she becomes the naked woman of the Star, free to pour out her water in all directions. Compare the six of Swords to the Fool.

The Fool's confidence, his leap into the sunshine would seem the complete opposite of the Swords card's dimness and acceptance. But

now notice that the Fool's stick appears as the ferryman's pole. For both, the blackness symbolizes potentiality. The Fool can go anywhere from his mountain, be anything. And the half-alive woman in the boat can choose her own destination.

The king of Pentacles reversed occupies the position of past experience. Right-side up the king of Pentacles signifies accomplishment and the satisfaction of success. In one hand he holds his sceptre, with the other he steadies his Pentacles on his knee. He looks down with pride at this symbol of his power. By his pose and his position as a figure of masculine authority he becomes a kind of stand-in for the Emperor (just as the queen of Pentacles' love of nature relates her to the Empress). Where the Emperor stresses the rule of law the king of Pentacles emphasizes achievement and the comfort and confidence produced by success and recognition. Upside-down it says that she has lacked these things in the past, and lacking them cannot overcome or escape the Emperor.

As mentioned above, the woman had worked in the arts and in healing. In none of these fields, however, had she achieved a significant public recognition. At the time of the reading she had begun to concentrate on her artistic work but remained unsure of what would come of it in practical terms. That is, she did not doubt her concepts or seriousness, only the chances of outward success. We also saw above that her father believed very strongly in the work ethic and financial success.

Without social recognition she believes herself weak, inadequate. She cannot stand up to the Emperor or become her own authority. She cannot shrug off society's and her father's (silent) condemnation of her as a failure. This condemnation is silent because she has absorbed it into herself. It fills the air of the silent six of Swords. In fact, her father did not actually condemn her. Loving his daughter he supported her in all she did. But inside herself, subconsciously, she believed she knew what he thought of people who could not point to material achievements. And so her sense of inadequacy becomes multiplied in her father's silence.

The silence about her work extends to herself. She does not consciously think of herself as inferior or her efforts as poor. But the feeling of inadequacy stays with her in the swords she carries in her boat. The king of Pentacles reversed as past experience brings it to consciousness.

Significantly we see the male head of the suit (the queen appears in the work cards as an alternative). With the Emperor as her centre she takes on the masculine view of maturity as confidence, power, social responsibility, possessions. Lacking these things she feels childlike, undeveloped. The king of Pentacles symbolizes important qualities (as the subject discovered in her meditation) but the card's values can stifle her as long as she sees them in terms of her own failure. She must first approach the suit through the queen before she can get a worthwhile sense of the king.

The three of Wands appeared as her expectation. This card had appeared in earlier readings where it usually expressed her hope of exploring the waters of new experience while keeping grounded in the realities of her life and accomplishments. Some of that meaning carries through here as well. The king of Pentacles signifies the lack of earth in her life, or perhaps the lack of a good relation to the things associated with that element. For if earth — the material world, work — becomes the desert of the Emperor, then she finds herself adrift in the waters of emotion. And without the kind of grounding shown in the three of Wands, she can only cover herself and keep the waters calm by silence. In the three, therefore, we see her desire for accomplishment and solidity so that she can begin to send out her own boat, rather than sit meekly in the ferry laden with swords.

But another meaning emerges from this card as well. In contrast to the Star, and in connection with the queen of Cups reversed (for right-side up the queen allows the water to merge into her dress) the three of Cups indicates a desire to explore the waters without getting wet. She recognizes the silence of the six of Swords, the boat that travels only in twilight, carrying shrouds to the land of the dead. She wants to send her boats into life. But she will stay behind, on the safe rock overlooking everything. Again we can compare this card to the (absent) Fool, willing to leap off his peak into whatever lies below. Water in the Tarot can often mean a willingness to dissolve the defensive ego in the formless energy of experience. Here the ego will insist on remaining a rock, an attitude picked up from the Emperor.

The first of the work cards advises her to stir up the waters and wet the lands. The Star holds nothing back. Symbol of true optimism she pours herself into all aspects of her being. Her emotions stimulate the unconscious waters so that they begin to ripple around her. At the same time she irrigates the Emperor's harsh land by her actions and her belief in the worth of those actions. If we lay the Major Arcana out as three lines of seven, then the Star comes two rows below the Empress. By not accepting the six of Swords and not taking the safe way of the three of Wands she can regain the Empress' quality of passion. But the Star goes beyond the third trump, for rather than envisioning passion in the outside world, or in the image of a mother's love, the Star says that she herself can experience joy in life.

Though the woman in the card places her foot on the water, it does not actually penetrate the surface. The pool symbolizes the unconscious which she can arouse without actually entering. In contrast to Judgement, whose resurrection out of the water makes it the direct opposite of the six of Swords, the Star does not really call for the ego to dissolve. Instead, it urges nakedness.

The queen of Pentacles also suggests the Empress. Like the trump she sits in a lush garden. A rabbit, symbol of fertility, runs along the lower right corner of the card. The queen represents the joy of nature, an appreciation of the gift of life. Where the king complacently pats his Pentacle the queen looks into hers, seeing the hidden magic of the physical world. The card tells her to enjoy life as it is, rather than viewing it through the eyes of the Emperor and finding it lacking. Instead of being troubled by her lack of the king she can cultivate the queen.

The Emperor involves dissatisfaction, for he demands that she compare her life now to some idea of the future. Inevitably she views herself as a failure for the Emperor is never satisfied, he is always better than we are. The queen of Pentacles allows her to experience herself. The queen is not passive or weak. Her straight back, her intense gaze into her pentacle, they give her a solidity. But she does not battle the world, or seek something beyond what exists. She looks within, entering into the heart of life.

The queen of Pentacles often means a woman to be trusted. As a work card it means she must learn to trust and respect who she is. Finding joy in her experience and surroundings she can learn to lure herself away from the condemnations of the internal Emperor, until she finds a new image, the queen of Earth. In contrast to the Emperor, an alien ruler, this image belongs to her, it is her, without that separation between herself and the power that controls her.

And the card means to trust her work as well, to believe in where it will take her. With its images of lush growth and fertility the queen of Pentacles symbolizes creativity, production. A strong connection exists between the queen and the Magician. It is first of all a connection of opposites, masculine Fire and feminine Earth. The greater the distance, the more things come together. If we see the Tarot as one long line, beginning with the Fool and ending with the king of Pentacles, then the Magician and the queen stand almost as far apart as possible. But if we join the ends into a circle, then the trump and the lady occupy the same position, one away from the link. We can see the connection in the colouring in the cards, the red and white robes, the yellow background. Both cards create, but they come at the act from opposite directions. The Fire needs to manifest itself in the world. It must ground itself in the things it produces. The queen of Pentacles begins with the Earth. She begins with her love for what exists now, and from that appreciation extends it by creating new things to give to the world. First she must believe in the value of her work, she must trust in its reality rather than judging it against some standard of social recognition.

The final work card takes her away from images of the Empress. At the same time it reinforces the idea of releasing burdens, and so reflects back on the other two cards. To the Star the ten of Wands reversed adds the idea that when she pours out the water she pours away her guilt. Similarly it emphasizes the aspect of freedom in the queen of Pentacles. Instead of carrying a pile of sticks to town she will sit in her garden.

The ten wands symbolize all the 'I should's' the woman lugs around with her. These include the notions of success, working hard (at a 'proper' job), making money, being a nice person, helping people, causing no distress to anyone, having the right kind of relationship, behaving 'properly' in public and in private, and so on and so on. Notice that even though the figure carries ten different sticks, they are all virtually the same. No matter how many particular variations 'I should' takes it always comes back to the same idea of a set of rules, a standard by which she always fails.

But the fact that there are many sticks remains important. Because the Emperor's standard splits up into many specific requirements she finds it that much harder to free herself of them. She can work against her guilt for one failure, convincing herself from her rational understanding that she has done nothing wrong, she's only lived her own life, but all the while the other requirements are bearing her down. The reading tells her she will not overcome guilt by analyzing the particular cases. She needs to change the mentality.

This message contains a danger of becoming yet another 'I should'. 'I should get rid of the Emperor. I should let go of my sense of failure. I should enjoy my life and trust my work.' The way to avoid such a trap lies partly in recognizing that work cards do not just advise what she should do, but what she can do. They tell her what lies available at this moment. And she can get out of the cycle by remembering that the cards do not advise a change of behaviour so much as a change of structure. The Star especially, but the other two cards as well, tell her she can break down the structure. She can release the water and let it flow into the dress of the queen of Pentacles.

In the woman's previous reading the ten of Wands appears as the outcome and the six of Swords as the possible outcome. Accepting the burdens has led to accepting the half-alive state of the boat. A connection exists between the ten sticks and the six of Swords. Both represent something she carries around with her. The Wands symbolize her conscious obligations, the Swords the sorrow and weight of guilt. The ten of Wands reversed as a work card suggests she can get rid of the swords through the step of dumping all those things she identifies as requirements.

The knight of Cups as her outcome represents an attempt at the release of the ten sticks. When we see, however, that she gets stuck there instead of a release it symbolizes a withdrawal, and its stillness evokes the dangerous silence of the six of Swords.

The woman chose a knight as her significator, an indication that she felt she had not established herself as an independent adult. Her choice of a forceful knight showed that she considered eagerness and courage among her best qualities. They are what liberates her from the stifling power of the Emperor. And yet, however far the knight of Wands ranges in his quest for adventure, he does not really escape the Emperor's pull. And when that pull exerts itself on him, the journey becomes muted, the eager cry silenced, the knight transformed into the cowled woman in the boat. In the knight of Cups we see her somewhere between these two states, a knight, but contemplative, withdrawn. But that contemplation does not lead to the queen.

Because the knight looks at his cup we can see some movement from the six of Swords, where she shrouded herself in a half-recognized despair and refused to disturb the swords. Here her emotions become transformed into the more benign image of the Cup, which she will hold up in front of her. And yet, the knight keeps a distance from his emotions. He contains them. Compare this image to the Star. She turns her gourds over, pouring out her feelings, pouring herself into her actions.

And compare him to the queen. Not at all passive, she evokes a female forcefulness far more powerful than any of the knights. The river flows into her dress, the same river which the Emperor tried to dam, which flows around the boat without wetting the woman, which runs before the knight's horse but does not touch him. The queen of Cups signifies the strength found in vulnerability. It appears upside-down because she fears to express this female power. She does not wish to separate herself from the Emperor. She does not wish to become herself.

Fulfilled, the queen of Cups would signify a further development of the queen of Pentacles as well as of the knight of Cups. Coming from the two female suits they embody the feminine archetype, but the queen of Cups goes beyond Pentacles enjoyment of the world. The Cups card brings out more fully the theme of creation implied by the queen of Pentacles' links to the Magician. Fulfilled, she would symbolize confidence and a way of achievement not bound up with the dominance and values of the Emperor. We have seen that the fourth trump represents a distorted image of her father, one which blocks her from accepting the love that he offers along with his fixed values. (The six of Swords shows a state in which love becomes damped down along with all other emotions.) But the queen of Cups is a card of love, and if she achieves the queen's independence then she can love her father as an equal, not a subject or competitor.

As with the earlier reading the reversed queen symbolized a potential as much as a failure. The question becomes how to bring out that potential. The work cards show her that the way lies through dissolving herself in the water, through loving the Earth and its passion, through dropping 'I should'. To help her in these things I suggested a series of meditations with a mandala from the reading. After some discussion we worked out the following pattern:

We placed the significator, the card of herself, beneath the mandala instead of in the middle because the pattern signifies what she wished to become, and therefore she needed to enter into it. The entry point becomes the ten of Wands reversed — the release of forced obligations. From there she can experience the Star and the queen of Pentacles and then through these reach the queen of Cups. The Star belongs on the left (the side of feeling) since it symbolizes internal states, while the queen of Pentacles stands for the outer reality of her life. The two come together in the queen of Cups. The movement thus becomes

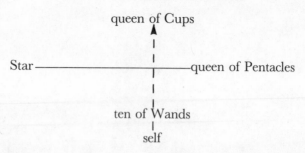

The dotted vertical line indicates that the ultimate movement is vertical, an evolution into a new state of being. The horizontal line reminds her that the Star and the queen of Pentacles are not isolated from each other. She does not split herself up going in both directions from the initial release of the ten of Wands reversed. By placing the significator below the mandala we leave the centre empty. Symbolically this says that she has not entered the centre of her own life, but remains outside, travelling through her life in the boat with the six swords. The blank spot also allows her to experiment with different images.

As mentioned earlier in the reading, to see the Emperor only as repression means blocking out the image's greater meaning of the laws and structures of existence. Eventually she should wish to achieve this greater view of the Emperor, but first she needs to free herself from the ruler as he exists in her mind. We decided that the trump belonged in the mandala, but not at first. The subject suggested she might add him later in place of the ten of Wands. In its beginning form the mandala emphasizes feminine values. It begins with her masculine self-image (knight of Wands) rejecting a masculine idea of burdens, and then moving to three female images. This strategy comes from the reading, where the male cards signified competition with the Emperor, while the female showed the possibility of alternatives. Of course such a stress on one side distorts the psyche. The return of the Emperor was designed partly to correct this imbalance. We will see that the trump did indeed enter the mandala, but in a different way, along with several other substitutes.

As with the earlier meditation I suggested a series of five. In this case the woman preferred to do them on successive days. Unlike the other subject she did not discuss them with me after each one, but kept a record which she has agreed to let me quote or paraphrase for this account. I will place any direct commentary of my own in parentheses.

On the first day she felt her way into the pattern. Concentrating

on the ten of Wands she said out loud, 'I release the burden of
.................'. She envisioned ten specific burdens and as she fixed each
one in her mind she let go of it. Finally she said out loud 'I am creative',
for the greatest burden she had carried was doubt.

On the second day she began to experiment. She added the king
of Pentacles in the centre. (By so doing she does more than restore
a masculine side. The king of Earth in the blank spot symbolizes the
possibility of achievement.) As if this action unlocked something each
of the cards became a wind. The north wind, the queen of Cups,
released her sense of being burdened by other people's demands. The
south wind, the ten of Wands reversed, released feelings of sexual
inadequacy. The east wind, the queen of Pentacles, released her lack
of inner discipline, while the west wind, the Star, released her rigidity.
When all the winds had blown on her she removed the ten of Wands
and replaced it, not with the Emperor, but with the king of Pentacles.
(Not with an outside force but with her own sense of confidence. The
action once more vacated the centre, leaving it open for new
possibilities.)

Now the winds blew again, but this time they brought her things
rather than taking things away. The north wind blew 'the wisdom
of the vision'. The south wind blew 'the fire of craftsmanship'. (Notice
that the change from the ten of Wands to the king of Pentacles
transforms sexual fears into art.) The east wind blew the 'inner
discipline of the spirit' while the west wind, the Star, 'blew the immortal
self bathing in the waters of life'. For her final act that day she picked
up the ten of Wands (she did not just put it away and forget about
it) and held it between her palms until the energy through her hands
dissolved all the blocks embodied in the card.

On the third day she picked up each of the four cards. She held
them and looked at them, and when she had absorbed each of them
she went through the Tarot deck until she found the Fool and added
the Fool to the centre. (As the number 0 the Fool symbolizes
nothingness, that is, freedom, the possibility to go anywhere, do
anything from where she is now. The Fool does not exist as a fixed
state of being like the other cards, and therefore does not take over
the centre, but in fact emphasizes its emptiness.) She picked up the
card for a closer look, then returned it to the pattern and sank more
deeply into her meditation. As she did so, she felt a surge of hope
and a belief in her ability to fulfil her wishes. She wrote 'Felt a
deepening of trust in myself.'

She began the fourth day by placing the nine of Swords in the centre
and then removing it. (In this way she experiments with removing

the six swords from the boat. By placing sorrow in the centre and discovering that nothing rises out of it — it produced no response — she frees herself from the anxiety of hidden pain. This trying-out is a valuable tool of the meditation. Through the introduction of semi-trance she places herself in an exposed state where the images of the Tarot trigger unexpected, or at least unplanned, reactions. If no such reactions occur then she can assume that the experiences summed up in that symbol are not relevant to her at this moment.)

She then replaced the king of Pentacles with the Fool. After absorbing this change she composed the following poem.

> I leap
>   I am leaping
>   I do leap
>
> The king is part of me
>   I leap.
> The king has a fool.
>   The fool leaps.
> The king stays on the throne
> The king is a fool.
>   The fool may be foolish
> The king leaps
>   The dog barks
>   I am the fool.

(The first three lines assert her identification with the image. Because she has allowed herself to slip into that muted half-life of the six of Swords she finds it difficult to believe she can jump free. Once she has done that she discovers that she does not need to deny the king of Pentacles, that is, the importance of achievement, of a place in society. She also realizes she can keep these values and still jump with the Fool.)

When she had written down the poem and returned to her meditation she found a great surge of anger rising in her. It seemed to her that she lived within barriers of rigid glass. She wrote

> If I were a wave I would uproot towers without a conscience.
> The Fool without the king is dangerous.
> He/She destroys the boundaries.
> She/He will awaken/awaken/awaken
> The Laws of Life change us

I am changing in ways I can't answer
I am tunneling under a distant sea
The moon is neither far nor foreign
You are near to me in another world
I can guess what I cannot finish
I too am torn, but the vision
    remains in all its beauty

('The Fool without the king is dangerous.' Dangerous for barriers
and repression, since the Fool breaks free. But dangerous for the soul
as well, for the soul needs structure and solidity. The Fool recognizes
only freedom. He does not fear the leap because he is weightless. But
we exist in our bodies, and we must learn to feel our weight in the
Earth. 'The Laws of Life change us'. Through the unification of the
Fool and the king of Pentacles in herself she discovers the true
Emperor, the laws that carry her beyond what she knows or can control
into a new land of the living.)

On the fifth day she created a new pattern.

She saw this as a six-pointed star which she called 'the fullness of life.' She then wrote about it, 'In the downward pointing triangle the Star and the Emperor come together in the vision/realizing intelligence of the queen of Cups.' (In the alchemical-hermetic symbol of the six pointed star the downward triangle symbolizes manifestation. As archetypes the Star and the Emperor reach back to the non-material 'world of forms'. Their very abstractness, however, makes them a proper base for the queen of Cups' solid reality. The connection asserts the origins of the material world in spirit.)

She wrote, 'The queen and king of Pentacles form the base of the upward pointing triangle. The four Wands are the top – breaking new ground in marriage.' (The upward triangle symbolizes spiritual growth. In the same sort of blending of opposites as the downward triangle she sees the base of growth as Pentacles — her achievements, her love of the world, her place in it. The four of Wands presents one of the Tarot's most striking images of liberation. The people leave the walled city to enter the simplest of constructions. As a four it provides an alternative to the repressive view of the Emperor — trump four — showing her that structure need not crush or imprison or close us off from the sunshine and the winds of life.

As a couple, the queen and king of Pentacles suggest 'marriage'. Commitment formed the basis of her relationship with her lover, but that commitment came from themselves, not from the traditional institution of marriage. Therefore they leave the Emperor's walled city to find their freedom in the Earth.)

Her final comment: 'The queen of Cups (her enactment of her own power, her re-discovery that love can break the silence) is the basis for my joy in the four of Wands.'

Chapter 4.

Meditation

Throughout these readings we have considered the possibility of using meditation to take the reading beyond information. In the two examples given, the particular cards used came from the reading itself. The purpose was to encourage developments or changes implied in the divination. But we can also use meditation to enter into the life of the Tarot and its archetypal images. This chapter consists of two transcripts of meditation exercises given by me to students in classes and workshops. I have taped them and copied them down just as they were done at the time, with brief instructions as to how to begin so that people with this book can recreate the exercise on their own. They can do so privately, taping the instructions and then playing them back, or they can form a group with one person speaking the meditation. Either way, readers can follow the examples as given, or, with some experimenting, create their own style and content. I hope that the transcripts will enable students to develop their own exercises for any cards that they may wish to explore.

The word 'meditation' can mean a number of different things. At one time in Christian culture it meant a private contemplation of some religious theme. This primarily rational concept of meditation still shows up in church sermons, or in retreats, or on religious broadcasts (non-evangelical) on radio and television. Far more common in the last few years is a concept of meditation derived from Zen masters and Indian gurus. In this sense the word means a release from all thoughts, as the self detaches from the ego and as much as possible from the external world. The techniques can vary, though they usually emphasize non-movement and concentration on the breath. Some teachers and organizations feature chanting, usually Indian songs or words. Most people in large cities have seen groups with shaven heads ringing bells as they parade through the shopping districts. One world-wide organization gives each of its members a secret word to chant over and over. But whether people sit motionless or dance, whether they sing or try to shake all thoughts out of their heads, this concept of meditation seeks to stop all mental activity, regarding thoughts, fantasies, and images primarily as illusions, and the release from them as liberation.

The type of meditation given in these examples — 'archetypal meditation' to coin a phrase — borrows some techniques from Eastern meditation, primarily the emphasis on breathing and relaxing the body, and the need to empty the mind of its normal glut of worries, plans, and memories. But these things all serve as steps towards a goal, rather than the goal itself. In archetypal meditation we seek to join ourselves to images. Knowing the power of the symbols to stimulate experience, and knowing that each card represents a different kind of experience we use meditation techniques to enter the archetypes. We join with them, we become part of their world of experience. When we meditate with the Magician we gain a sense of creative power. When we meditate with the High Priestess we give ourselves the chance to know a stillness and an inner truth that cannot be broken up and described. With the Hanged Man we glimpse the connectedness of all things, and with certain Minor cards we confront the unknown areas, the wildness, just beyond the boundaries of ordinary life.

Now, of course these transformations do not occur the moment we sit down with the card before us and start breathing deeply. The stimulation, the openings, can come very slowly. We may have to go back to the image a number of times, or many times, slowly working our way in before we feel ourselves part of the archetype. But the cards remain. They form a system independent of personal fantasies, however much we invest them with our own experiences. And because they remain, because they come to us as objects we can hold in our hands and lay in front of us, we can keep returning to them in meditations and other exercises as well as in readings. The more we return, the more energy we put into the archetypes, the more power they gain to work on us and draw us into them. For just as the archetypes exist independent of us they also come to life through the effort we put into them. As you meditate with the Sun its universal meanings take on the particular colour of your life, of everything you give to it.

Sometimes one card may take on a very personal quality. An artist might identify her creative ambitions with the Magician. Her meditation with the card will become a way to realize her power. When she feels weak or blocked she can bring the image of the Magician to her mind, and because of all she's experienced with the card she can use it to burn away her doubts in the creative flame. Or a man under a lot of pressure might use the Hanged Man to connect himself to something more fundamental than daily irritants.

In the first Celtic cross reading we saw how Justice so symbolized the subject's goals and hopes that it became his personal archetype. Meditation would have strengthened this connection, giving the image greater power to help him become what he wanted to become. In this sort of meditation the person deliberately seeks to 'charge' the card with aspects of the self. Then, when he enters the card, those aspects become amplified, energized by the symbol. They return to him with greater power to affect his life.

The two meditations given here are less personal, meant to apply to anyone wishing to enter the Tarot's archetypal world. As mentioned above the method borrows techniques from Eastern meditation. It also takes qualities from the occult tradition of astral travelling and from the guided fantasies used in some psychotherapy. It differs, however, from all of these.

Occultists tend to see the cards as keys to distinct realms of existence. These realms contain definite characteristics (including sometimes lists of angels, demons, archons, etc.). Through the entering of a trance they attempt to detach themselves from their bodies and move into these alien countries. 'Archetypal' meditation, as I have called it, does not aim for such a radical departure. The subject remains conscious and remains in the body. Indeed, part of the goal is to bring an awareness of the symbol into the body, so that some exercises (not included here) include movements or postures.

In regard to guided fantasies, archetypal meditation will often use techniques of setting the person within the scene of the card and then allowing the situation to come to life. The person sees how the situation develops, what actions take place, what responses come up. To do this requires a certain passivity produced by relaxation and breathing exercises. We do not decide which way we want the story to develop, but allow it to follow its own course, without analysis. Only later, after the meditation, do we consider what it means. In a class once, I used a tree fantasy for the Hanged Man, and told people to climb the tree, observing what it looked like, what they saw along the way, and so on. One woman experienced the tree as barren, empty of leaves or moss. If she had planned the fantasy ahead of time she would not have chosen such an image. But the barren tree appeared to her, and because it did, it enabled her to face certain facts about her life. She told me afterwards that the meditation led her to make a decision she had been putting off for months.

Sometimes the leader of a group will create some scene or story that suggests the qualities of the card without actually depicting the picture. In the last reading in this book we referred to a meditation done by someone else using the Emperor. In that exercise, the subject (and I) set a scene of a wide plain with a great many people working for the Emperor. A number of times in workshops the members experienced the Hanged Man through the fantasy mentioned above — that of climbing the world tree.

Fantasies, however, form only one technique of meditation. Often it is enough to enter into the card and feel its qualities. Action within the scene is not always necessary. And even when we do use fantasies, guided or spontaneous, the emphasis lies not on personal development or working out specific problems but on the image, the archetypes. We do these meditations not to strengthen the ego or overcome fears, or confront obsessions, or any of the other therapeutic purposes of fantasies. We do them to experience the different ways of being, the varying mysteries, evoked by the cards.

Meditation for a purpose does have its place with the Tarot. (Both the examples that follow serve the 'purpose' of detaching the self from external experiences.) We have seen in the two mandala meditations how we can enter the cards to get past difficulties shown in the reading. But even there the emphasis moves away from the ego and self-awareness to a focus on the symbols and the play between them. The subject of the last reading did not put herself into the archetypes so much as allow them to enter her. And so they became winds blowing on her, freeing her from anxieties and doubts.

For many people fantasy meditations suggest conquering fears — the 'heroic ego' as some psychologists have called it. We set up a scene representing some problem symbolically and then the person comes in as a champion or knight to kill the dragon, or descend into the cave and find the treasure or climb the mountain to free the princess. Thus the ego becomes stronger through defeating its enemies. But there are other ways of being than heroism and the needs of the soul are not necessarily those of the ego. In recent years a number of pyschologists, notably Mary Watkins and James Hillman, have challenged the assumptions of conquest, seeing the hero as a kind of patriarchal fixation. As Watkins suggests, maybe we should let the dragon win and see what *that* does for us.

If we take this non-heroic, non-directed course, we should recognize an important point about archetypal meditation. We must not fear what emerges from it. Many people believe that if their fantasies bring up monsters or disease or sexual strangeness or violence or humiliation, then they have uncovered some terrible secret about themselves. But in fact we all encompass many personalities, and no one side of us invalidates the rest. More important, we should recognize that the unconscious speaks through its own vocabulary. Hillman has stressed that the unconscious gains our attention through bizarre, or 'pathological', images. In a sense, our fantasies do not 'belong' to us at all, but to the language of the imagination.

In Tarot meditation we shift attention away from ourselves to the symbols. And because these symbols are so varied when we enter them they bring us into a wide array of existences. Through the play of symbols, from the light of the Magician and the darkness of the High Priestess, through surrender to Death or the primal fears of the Moon, through the exploration of the three of Wands or the disciplined spirit of the nine of Pentacles, we encounter our many selves as well as the world in all its wonders.

General Instructions
Preparation for these meditations is simple. Choose a time and a place where you will feel comfortable and will not be disturbed by visitors or external noises. If you are doing the meditation at night, use only a dim light; if in the day, however, it should not be necessary to block out the sunlight.

Wear loose clothes and sit or lie down in a comfortable position with the back straight. If sitting you should try not to draw the knees up to the chest. This will restrict your breathing. If you can, sit on the floor with your legs crossed. If not, fine. But make sure you choose a position where you do not have to move around often. Some people prefer to sit on a cushion with the back braced against the wall. Others sit in a straight backed chair or lie on the floor without a pillow.

If you think you might want to end the exercises by writing something in a journal or drawing a picture or holding some object (such as the tree branch in the Hermit meditation from the last Celtic cross reading) place these things beside you ahead of time so you will not have to break your mood by looking for them.

Before you begin the meditation itself take the card in your hand and look at the picture. Focus on it, the images, the symbols, even the colours and the feel of the card as an object. Use this focusing as a separation from your previous thoughts and actions. Then place the card in front of or beside you, close your eyes, and begin.

A Note on the Transcripts

When speaking or taping these instructions try to talk slowly and quietly, without whispering or distorting your natural tones. The voice should function as an instrument of relaxation and a guide through the meditation.

The transcripts include spaces between parts of the instructions. These mirror pauses taken during the actual event, when the people taking part were given the chance to absorb and experience each phase before going on to the next. Each meditation took approximately half an hour. Some experimenting will give an indication of how much time to leave between sections.

MEDITATION ONE — THE FOOL

Begin by feeling yourself sitting peacefully and calmly.

Begin to let your breathing open out. Allow your breathing to become longer and gentler, and slowly let your breathing go deeper . . . as you take your breath into your centre, into your diaphragm, and let it out gently.
And as you do, feel yourself relax.

With each breath feel your body become more relaxed and more calm. And as you breathe in, breathe in relaxation into your body and peacefulness. And as you breathe out breathe away your thoughts, and your worries, and your tensions.

Feel your body begin to relax. Allow the top of your head to relax, your forehead, and feel the relaxation move down to your eyes. Let go of all the tension around your eyes and the bridge of your nose. Just let it release as you breathe.

Let your cheeks relax, and your mouth, and your jaw. Let all the tensions around your jaw and your mouth relax. Just let them go out of your body.

Begin to feel like the Fool, free and peaceful.

Let your shoulders relax, let them loose, and the upper arms, and the elbows, down your arms, let your fingers relax.

Let your breastbone relax, and your upper back. Feel the relaxation move down through your chest, to your centre . . . to your hips . . . feel it move through your legs, your thighs, to your knees, to your calves, all the way down to your toes.

As your body relaxes be aware only of your breath. With each breath in, you are at peace. As you breathe out breathe away again all the thoughts and worries that try to crowd in on your mind.

And as you breathe, as your mind tries to fill up with interferences and distractions, keep the image of the Fool in place. And let the feeling of the Fool, the feeling of the card and the picture, free you from all your distractions.

And as you breathe deeper into your feeling of peace, and quiet, and joy, allow yourself to realize that you can become free of all the different follies, all the problems and worries that have built up in you over the years.

Feel the way the Fool can free you from the things that have built up over the years. Allow yourself to release your troubles and worries. As you breathe in breathe in a sense of calm and peace, so that nothing can harm you or touch you. And as you breathe out feel that your breath is like the dance of the Fool. It can carry away your troubles and your worries, your anxieties, and fears.

Now do the same with your thoughts and ideas. As you breathe in, breathe in a sense of freedom. A sense of endless possibilities. And as you breathe out let the dance of the Fool carry away your ideas, all the conceptions you've built up, all the thoughts that try to crowd in on you.

Let it carry away even your ideas about the Fool.

Let all the ideas that have seemed important to you float away.

Now do the same with all those things that you feel make up you, all the qualities, the ideas, feelings that over the years you've come to believe are what you are. Let these things float away on your breath.

And as you breathe in you realize that you are something else. Something free, not attached to all the qualities and beliefs that have built up over time.

And as you breathe out let go of these things. Let go of all the things you once would have said were you.

Feel instead the freedom and joy of the life of the Fool.

And as you experience this feeling of purity and peace allow yourself to realize that all your troubles and all your thoughts are nothing. They do not exist. They are only an illusion. They are nothing.

Feel that the room, the floor you are sitting on, is nothing. Any noises, everything around you, is nothing. Any distractions that try to enter you, remember that they are nothing. You can breathe them away, they can float away from you with your breath. And realize that you are nothing. Just as your thoughts are nothing . . . and the environment that surrounds you is nothing . . . so you are nothing. There is only peace and joy and freedom.

And these are also nothing.

Let this nothingness become a circle of light.

Allow yourself to see and feel this shining circle of light . . . radiant and beautiful.

From this circle of light let your awareness descend to a mountaintop. A very beautiful mountaintop in the bright sunlight. Feel the clean air, the warmth of the sun, see the other mountaintops around you, snow-covered, pure.

Feel yourself free, to dance on the mountaintop. And as you dance remember still that the mountain is nothing. The sky, the sun are nothing. They are only part of your dance.

From your mountaintop feel that you can go anywhere, enter into anything. From nothing you can become anything.

And now in a moment you will slowly, peacefully, open your eyes. Before you you will find a pad of paper and some pens. You will take a sheet of paper, or several, however many you need, and a pen, and draw or write something of your experience being with the Fool and with nothingness.

And keep your feeling of peace and freedom as you open your eyes and take the paper and the pen.

MEDITATION TWO —
THE EIGHT OF CUPS

Let yourself become comfortable.

Let yourself get a position where you don't have to move. Close your eyes and relax. Let your body settle, let your breathing begin to lengthen out, become more natural, less forced.

Let yourself breathe from deep in your centre, from your diaphragm, and as you breathe begin to relax.

With each breath in breathe calm and peace into your body. And with each breath out breathe away all thoughts and tensions and worries that are filling your mind.

And as you breathe in let your breathing begin to relax your body. Breathe in relaxation, breathe away all tensions.

Slowly let relaxation move down your body. Let the top of your head relax, let your hair relax, let your forehead relax . . . let your ears relax, and your eyes, let all the tension around your eyes release from your body. And the bridge of your nose, and your nose, and your cheek, let the relaxation move down to your mouth, and your lips, and your jaw, all the tension that you carry in your jaw let your breath carry it away, softly out of your body.

Feel the relaxation move down your neck, to your throat, to your shoulder, let your shoulders drop, let everything out, feel the relaxation move down your chest, feel your body relax, feel your diaphragm relax as you move deeply.

And your belly, and your stomach.

And let your arms relax, your shoulders, down your arms to your elbows, down your hands to your fingertips.

Feel the wonderful relaxation fill your body with every breath.

Feel your hips relax, and your groin, feel your buttocks relax, your thighs, and your knees, and down your legs to your feet, all the way to your toes, your whole body relaxing.

And now as you breathe let the sense of relaxation, of peace, deepen in your body. With each breath feel yourself more and more in your self. With each breath out release all the thoughts, and all the extraneous information that tries to fill up your mind. Let your breath gently carry them away.

As you breathe in feel yourself going deeply into yourself. And as you breathe out, breathing away whatever is extraneous, feel yourself go still more deeply into yourself. At peace and relaxed.

And from deep within yourself, imagine yourself in a quiet place at the bottom of a hill. The sun is shining, in front of you is a small stream of water. Let yourself be in this place, feeling relaxed, and warm and pleasant, and feel the strength of the sun . . . and the peacefulness as you stay with your breath and the sense of yourself in this warm pleasant place.

And now, in front of you, notice a group of cups . . . quite large, and attractive, bright colours. Allow yourself to peacefully get up and go toward the cups, to begin to pick them up and arrange them in a nice orderly way.

Feel their weight . . . see what they look like, feel the size and the texture. Just as you feel the sun, just as you can hear and see the stream of water flowing before you.

And as you arrange the cups in a certain way, in a nice orderly way, allow yourself to look inside them.

And see in them all the different known things in your life. The things you know and have done in your life.

Some of them will show your accomplishments, the things you've made and done and built up in your life.

Allow yourself to see these things in the cups, the things you have made in your life.

And other cups or the same cups, will show you your hopes.

And some of them will show you your fears.

And some will show you your fantasies.

Allow yourself to look in these cups, feeling at peace with yourself. Let yourself look peacefully at your hopes, and fears, and fantasies.

And now, in some of the cups, or the same cups, see your relationships with other people and with yourself. See in the cups the relationships you've built up in your life, what you've made of them, and what they've made of you.

Now let yourself step back from the cups. And as you step back, look at them again, and see again in the cups your accomplishments, what you've done in your life, and your hopes, and your fears, and your fantasies, and your relationships, and the things you've made of yourself. And realize that all these things that you know, that have happened, are not you. You are something more, and deeper, than all these things in the cups.

And as you sit down again, facing the cups, once again feel a sense of peace as you return to your breathing. And a sense of knowing that the things in the cups are very valuable and wonderful, but they are still apart from you yourself.

And as you settle into your breathing again, with a sense of peace in yourself, allow darkness to come over the sky. A peaceful darkness, so that the moon appears instead of the sun. Under the light of the moon you feel a deep sense of quiet, a sense of well-being, a feeling of being inside yourself and at peace with yourself.

And with this sense of peace allow yourself to slowly get up and begin to walk up the hill under the light of the moon. Let the calm light of the moon shine on you as you slowly walk up the hill, leaving behind the eight cups, leaving behind all the things you have known and have made in the past as you walk quietly under the moon.

As you walk up the hill feel yourself with yourself and in yourself, a sense of wholeness as you leave behind the things you have known as you walk towards the mystery.

And recognize that this journey you have taken, under the moon, in the dim light, this journey into the unknown, is a journey you will take many times in your life. Many times, when you wish, or when it is right for you, you will enter into yourself, and leave behind the cups of the things you have known, and walk peacefully into the unknown.

And know as well that whenever you feel yourself too attached to the things in your life, to your accomplishments, or your hopes, or your fears, or your fantasies, or too attached to your relationships, and you wish to separate yourself, to be with yourself, you have only to remember this walk under the moon, and to remember the image of the eight of Cups from the Tarot. And this image will return you to yourself and to the mystery.

Now pick up the card before you and press it against your body, so that you feel the image become a part of you.

And now that you have had this experience, and have joined yourself to the image, when you feel ready open your eyes.

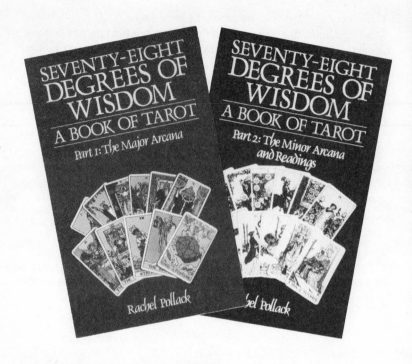

SEVENTY-EIGHT
DEGREES OF WISDOM

A BOOK OF TAROT

Part 1: The Major Arcana

Rachael Pollack. *Illustrated.* A psychological approach to the Tarot, examining all aspects of the cards — their origins, symbolism, and their historical, mythological and esoteric background. Author uses the 1910 A. E. Waite Tarot as her primary source because it allows the pictures to work on the subconscious:

Part 2: The Minor Arcana and Readings

Rachael Pollack. *Illustrated.* The long-awaited sequel to Rachael Pollack's widely-praised analysis of the Major Arcana of the Tarot. Here she examines in depth the Minor Arcana (with particular reference to the Rider-Waite deck) and demonstrates readings of the combined Major and Minor Arcana. Gives many illuminating insights into the complexities of Tarot divination.